Wearing the Morning Star

NATIVE AMERICAN SONG-POEMS

Brian Swann

WITH A PREFACE BY THE AUTHOR

UNIVERSITY OF NEBRASKA PRESS
LINCOLN AND LONDON

This book is for Roberta,
with love

Preface © 2005 by the Board of Regents of the University of Nebraska
Manufactured in the United States of America

∞

First Nebraska paperback printing: 2005

Library of Congress Cataloging-in-Publication Data
Wearing the morning star: Native American song-poems / [edited by]
Brian Swann; with a preface by the author.
p.   cm.
Originally published: New York: Random House, c1996.
Includes bibliographical references.
ISBN-13: 978-0-8032-9340-3 (pbk.: alk. paper)
ISBN-10: 0-8032-9340-2 (pbk.: alk. paper)
1. Indian poetry—North America—Translations into English.   I. Swann,
Brian.
PM197.E3W43   2005
897—dc22   2005009172

PREFACE

As I noted in the original introduction that follows this preface, the "song-poems" in this book are not my translations. I have not worked with the original languages.[1] So what are they, or, to put it another way, what are they not? They are not "imitations"—"licensed liveliness" in the tradition of Ezra Pound and Robert Lowell (or even Jerome Rothenberg).[2] Nor are they "metaphrase" or "paraphrase," two other translation categories that Dryden distinguishes in his preface to the translation of Ovid's *Epistles* (1680). I prefer simply to call my freeverse reworkings of scholarly originals "song-poems," even though they include what we call the sacred, while "song" usually implies the secular. In addition, "song-poem" is something of an oxymoron. Music's effect, like that of scent, is dependent on something ineffable. Take this away and what is left is attenuated.

To complicate matters somewhat, confusion has recently arisen over what exactly "poetry" means in a Native American context, especially since the term has been extended to narratives in "prose." Some scholars (mostly linguists) reject this poetics, preferring to stick with Franz Boas's "austere linguistic purism." For them "interlinear glossing" is the most congenial choice, even though the results often prove virtually unreadable.[3] The other camp adapts or adopts the work of Dell Hymes, who has uncovered a variety of organizing principles and patterns in oral narratives that allow him to call them "poetry."[4]

Early collectors, however, had no doubts about what poetry was. They simply incorporated songs into the already available genre of "poetry." By the end of the nineteenth century, the pioneering Theodore Baker had set the stage for George Cronyn, Mary Austin, Grove Day, and others by using the term without seeing the need for much discussion. For him it was enough to qualify the songs as poetry if they possessed "rhythmic feeling," "an abundance of most beautiful images borrowed directly from nature," and "natural power of feeling."[5]

All this is by way of background to what I have attempted to do. I have aimed throughout at "decorum," in its original sense of that which is fitting, right, and appropriate. I wanted the song-poems to be as accessible as possible. What I have tried to do is reanimate and reclothe the transcriptions, and in the process involve the reader who is encouraged, via notes and sources, to participate in the process of re-creation. During this process I have always been aware of the problem of "authenticity." Barry O'Connell has noted that "authenticity is a seductive illusion in this cultural area."[6] In a field shot through with difficult ambiguities, where "authenticity" is impossible, I have nevertheless sought to be as responsible and "authentic" as I can be.

I decided not to add more song-poems to this new edition because, for the most part, I had already selected those that appealed to me for this volume and its predecessor, *Song of the Sky*. However, for the last few years I have been working with Dell Hymes, who had been working with the Algonquian linguist John Nichols, on retranslating one of the best-known and most anthologized of Native American songs, a song that Frances Densmore collected from the Ojibwe and published early in the last century.[7] It seems she made some mistakes in her translation, but I will spare the reader the voluminous back and forth among the translators over this tiny song, titled by Densmore "A Song of Spring." She broke the original nine phrases thus:

As my eyes
search
the prairie
I feel the summer in the spring.

Here is the Nichols/Hymes/Swann version (which attempts a more "concrete" approach):

For

    I will explore

                     all the prairie

   now   spring hints

                       summer

    everywhere.

(Sadly, I cannot say that I prefer the more accurate version to the older version. I still have a soft spot for Densmore's translation, no doubt because it was one of the first Native American "poems" I came across many years ago as I was starting out in something like my own spring-summer.)

Finally, I would like to thank all those at the University of Nebraska Press. I especially want to express my gratitude to Gary Dunham, director, who has been most kind and helpful with this book and others. I dedicate this book, once more, to my wife Roberta for her love, support, and generosity of spirit.

NOTES TO PREFACE

1. In the introduction I refer the reader to my *Coming to Light* (1993) for new translations of songs by language experts. To this I should add my *Voices from Four Directions: Contemporary Translations of the Native Literatures of North America* (University of Nebraska Press, 2003), which contains San Juan Pueblo Turtle Dance songs and O'odham Whirlwind songs. Other songs are found in *Algonquian Spirit: Contemporary Translations of the Algonquian Literatures of North America* (University of Nebraska Press, 2005). It includes Passamaquoddy social and Wampum ceremonial songs and Arapaho Ghost Dance songs.

2. The phrase "licensed liveliness" is from Robert M. Adams, *Proteus, His Lies, His Truth* (Norton, 1973), 96.

3. Victor Golla, "Editorial Notes," *SSILA Newsletter* 23, no. 2 (July 2004): 2.

4. A concise statement of Hymes's position can be found in his short essay "Poetry" in the *Journal of Linguistic Anthropology* 9, no. 1–2 (2000), 191–93. For a brief but wide-ranging discussion of the topic see Robert Bringhurst's Belcourt lecture, "Prosodies of Meaning: Literary Form in Native North America," published in 2004 by Voices of Rupert's Land (Linguistics Department, University of Manitoba, Winnipeg, Canada).

5. Baker, 69. See introduction note 7 for bibliographic details.

6. Foreword to Brian Swann, *Song of the Sky: Versions of Native American Song-Poems* (University of Massachusetts Press, 1993), 17.

7. Frances Densmore, *Chippewa Music*, 2 vols. (Da Capo Press, 1972), originally published as Bulletin 45 (1910) and Bulletin 53 (1913) of the Bureau of American Ethnology, Smithsonian Institution. This song can be found in volume 2 on page 254. At Red Lake in northern Minnesota, Densmore used her phonograph to collect the song from Ajidegujig ("an old man who wears his hair in long braids"). She notes that it was "composed in dream" during a "fasting vigil," and that after it had been sung it became tribal property, to be used in war dances.

"My children, my children,
it is I who wear the morning star on my head."

—Arapaho Ghost Dance Song

//////////////////////////////////////

CONTENTS

CONTENTS

//////////////////////////////////////

INTRODUCTION

UNTIL THE MID–NINETEENTH century there was little interest in North America in recording the songs, dances, and ceremonies of the native peoples.[1] To the first Europeans—Puritans, French Jesuits, and Spaniards alike—the native religions represented a satanic threat. The Europeans regarded the ceremonies as hellish and heard the songs as mere yelling. Thus in the seventeenth century Paul Le Jeune wrote about a Huron feast, "I believe that if the demons and the damned were to sing in hell, it would be after this fashion," and Pierre Roubaud found Abnaki singing "the cries and howling of wolves."[2] This attitude persisted for the next three hundred years. In the introduction to his *Navajo Legends* of 1897, a book which provided a new perspective for a public that had rarely been exposed to positive accounts of Native American culture, Washington Matthews quotes a letter written by an army physician and published in the *Smithsonian Report* for 1855. "Their music," says Jonathan Letterman, "is but a succession of shrieks, and is anything but agreeable."[3] (He also repeats the age-old calumny that Indians had no religion and no tradition, but he didn't go as far as Columbus, who claimed they had no language.)[4]

In the nineteenth century it was widely believed that Indians were about to pass from the scene of history via Manifest Destiny, the natural order of Darwinian progress, or some other popular and convenient doctrine. Notions such as these, together with the attempted destruction of the native way of life, made the collection of cultures before they disappeared a matter of some urgency. Native American stories, songs, and ceremonies began to be taken more seriously. Not that they were regarded as having much value in themselves. The collecting of these materials was meant to provide, as in the case of Henry Rowe Schoolcraft, access to the Indian's soul, necessary for converting Indians to Christianity. Or the materials provided evidence of "man's rise to civilization," up the evolutionary scale from the Indians' "child race" to the nineteenth-century white man.

In the mid–nineteenth century, German scholars such as Carl Stumpf and Erich M. von Hornbostel had begun the field collection of folk music, aided by the invention of the phonograph, and had taken an interest in Native American music. Their work laid the foundations of a sound methodology for the study of this music.[5] Some Americans picked up this interest and used similar techniques. During the years 1889 to 1890, Jesse Walter Fewkes did fieldwork with the Zuni and Passamaquoddy, recording their songs on Edison cylinders, thus making these peoples the first non-Western musicians ever to be recorded.[6] When the young American Theodore Baker wanted to study Native American music he went to Germany. His *On the Music of the North American Indians* began life as a doctoral dissertation at Leipzig University, and was based on a summer's fieldwork in 1880 on the Seneca Reservation in New York and at Carlyle Indian School ("Training School for Indian Youth at Carlyle, PA"). When published in 1882 it became the first book of its kind.[7] At the end of the nineteenth century and into the twentieth, pioneering work was being done in the field by Washington Matthews, Alice Fletcher, in collaboration with the Osage Francis La Flesche, Frances Densmore, H. R. Voth, and others. The work of Franz Boas is often seen as representing a break with the past, though the extent of this break has been exaggerated. What Boas does represent is a new "scientific" approach to gathering, translating, and interpreting materials, a break with evolutionism, and a respect for the integrity of the cultures, taking them, as much as possible, on their own terms. Boas can legitimately be called the father of American anthropology as a professional discipline. Many of the other great figures of twentieth-century American anthropology, such as Alfred Kroeber, Ruth Benedict, George Herzog, Edward

Sapir, Ruth Bunzel, and Robert Lowie, were his students at Columbia University.

Interest in the music itself was being developed by such scholars as Benjamin Ives Gilman and John Comfort Fillmore, and a good number of composers began using the collections of songs made by Densmore, Fletcher, and others; they set about incorporating (or co-opting) the music in accordance with a nationalistic agenda. If Schoolcraft's purpose, first outlined in *Algic Researches* of 1839 (the first study to collect and extensively analyze Native American materials), was to convert Indians to Christianity, the main idea behind the activities of these composers was that America needed its own musical tradition; it needed to mine its own "native national wealth."[8]

Folk music had begun to be part of the national musics of Europe. In 1892, the arrival of Antonín Dvořák in New York to teach and conduct provided a boost for those who wished to establish a truly American musical art. Dvořák, who left the United States in 1895, tried to get American composers to use American materials. "The new American music must strike its roots deeply into its own soil," he wrote in the *New York Herald*, 28 May 1893. In his 1893 Symphony No. 9, *From the New World*, he put what he preached into practice. The Largo and other sections were probably inspired by Longfellow's *The Song of Hiawatha* (1855), and by Dvořák's own testimony the Scherzo was inspired by "Hiawatha's Wedding Feast." *The Song of Hiawatha* was, in turn, largely based on the work of Schoolcraft. (Dvořák himself had heard Native American music, probably central Algonquin or Iroquois, when on vacation in Iowa, and he received transcriptions of Iroquois songs from Henry Krehbiel, a New York critic. He also read available ethnographies.)

So composers, with the aim of creating a national music that was non-European in origin, set off in pursuit of "the musical soul of the Indian," as one of them, Thurlow Lieurance, phrased it.[9] But when captured it needed to be "idealized," to use the term employed by another of these composers, Charles Wakefield Cadman. This involved harmonizing and forcing the music into the twelve-tone Western system. He wished to treat "the folk-songs in terms of modern musical thought consonant with the present musical style."[10]

Frederick R. Burton, composer of the opera *Hiawatha* and other pieces, is quite candid about what we might now call his assimilationist and imperialist aesthetic. He is adapting the songs, he says, "for the uses of civilization," and urges "patriotism" on fellow composers. On the "primitive stock" they should graft their "art." They should forget the music's origin and "proceed according to the purely musical demands of the subject."[11] Since he assumed that Indians would not last much longer, he thought the work was of some urgency. (We should remember that this was a time of great hardship for native peoples; the General Allotment Act, or Dawes Act, of 1887 had extinguished Indian title to millions of acres of land in an all-out effort to "break up the tribal mass," destroy Indian cultures, and free up land for white settlers.) Burton urged "the preservation of *our* primitive music while it yet lingers in the memory of Indian singers"[12] (my italics). He believed he was dealing with "the beginnings of music," since Indians, in his evolutionary scheme, possess "a low, or rather, undeveloped order of intelligence." But Indians would not be allowed to complete the process of artistic development by themselves. That will be undertaken on their behalf by the white man, since he has a true aesthetic sense and knows real "artistic values" and "permanent value." He will provide the methods by which Indian song can transcend its origin.[13] Other composers who belonged to this movement include Edward Mac-Dowell (generally credited with the first use of Indian themes in American concert music, themes obtained from Theodore Baker's book; his *Indian Suite* was first performed in 1896), Arthur Nevin, Carl Busch, Eastwood Lane, H. W. Loomis, Homer Grun, Charles Skilton, Carlos Troyer, and Arthur Farwell, founder of the Wa-Wan Press, established primarily to publish works by composers who were developing specifically American themes. He encouraged American composers to use Native American songs in place of borrowed European (in particular German) melodies.

If this was the "high" end of the appropriation of Indian music, at the other end was a proliferation of Indian music for schools and for various community groups. Indian music was meant to be assimilated in diluted form by white people, especially children. Indian songs and ceremonies were reduced to children's games, as Indian life itself was soon to be reduced to Cowboys and Indians on the silver screen. Frequently the two ends were linked by the same people, including Frances Densmore and Alice Fletcher.[14] Thus in 1921 Densmore published *Indian Action Songs*, "A Collection of Descriptive Songs of the Chippewa Indians, with Directions for Pantomimic Representation in Schools and Community Assemblies," and Fletcher wrote *Indian Games and Dances with Native Songs* about the same time. "It will appeal especially to Camp Fire Girls and Boy Scouts," the jacket copy announced.[15]

Interest in the songs as *poetry* existed alongside interest in the songs as music. Again, this interest was stimulated by the desire to create a new and genuinely American art. In 1907, Natalie Curtis published the still valuable *The Indians' Book*, the first anthology of myth, music, and song. It was meant to help the Indians, "to revive for the younger generation the sense of the dignity and worth of their race which is the Indians' birthright, and without which no people can progress."[16] Curtis also noted that Indian song (sometimes, following European practice, she called it "folk music") possessed something essential, something missing from the American spirit. "However crude," it was an art of sincere and spontaneous impulses, she claimed. "The undeveloped talents native to the aboriginal American are precisely those in which the Anglo-Saxon is deficient."[17]

Mary Austin was the leading figure in the movement to rejuvenate American poetry through the absorption of the "aboriginal" American spirit. In *The American Rhythm: Studies and Reexpressions of Amerindian Songs* (1923) she called for this renewal via a close relationship with the American earth and its indigenous inhabitants. This poetry would be characterized by an open or free form, an organic rhythm, and a stress on the incantatory and imagistic. (The story of the relationship between American poetry and Native American song is told in detail by Michael Castro in *Interpreting the Indian: Twentieth-Century Poets and the Native*

American [University of New Mexico Press, 1983], and my account is indebted to him.)

"Reexpressions" of Native American song began to appear frequently in magazines in the first decade of this century, culminating in 1917 with the aboriginal issue of the prestigious magazine *Poetry*. "The first authoritative volume of aboriginal American verse," as Mary Austin called it in her introduction to the volume, was George Cronyn's *The Path on the Rainbow: An Anthology of Songs and Chants from the Indians of North America* (1918), which included work from leading ethnographers. But we had to wait for over thirty years before two other major anthologies appeared: Margot Astrov's *The Winged Serpent: An Anthology of American Indian Prose and Poetry* (1946) and A. Grove Day's *The Sky Clears: Poetry of the American Indians* (1951). In the 1960s, the magazine *Alcheringa*, under the editorship of Jerome Rothenberg and Dennis Tedlock, created "ethnopoetics." Its pages were home to adaptations and reexpressions, as well as translations, of "tribal poetries" from all over the world. When Rothenberg's *Shaking the Pumpkin* came out in 1971, "America was going through a spell of Indianismo."[18] Rothenberg's "total translation," his "continuing experiment with ways to translate the native poetries into English,"[19] has been criticized for the liberties it takes, but perhaps it is helpful to follow Arnold Krupat by seeing Rothenberg's work not so much in the context of "translation" as in the context of "ethnocriticism."[20] Rothenberg's most recent ideas on translation can be found in his essay " 'We Explain Nothing, We Believe Nothing': American Indian Poetry and the Problematics of Translation."[21]

The poems in this book, the "song-poems," are not my translations[22] since I have not worked with the original languages. They are based on translations. Sometimes the original translators (e.g., Knut Bergsland, Linda Goodman and Peter Garcia, Leanne Hinton and David McAllester) looked over what I had done with their work. I am grateful for their help.

Unlike my previous book of "versions," *Song of the Sky*, I have not tried to be predominantly "concrete" in my approach to making poems out of the songs, prayers, and ceremonies, but when the material seemed to call for it I have made a number of gestures in a plastic or kinetic direction, since I feel it helps to lift the words a little, off the page, back into the air, back into performance, into their oral nature. Unlike in *Song of the Sky*, however, there are no typographical tours de force such as the "Yuma Deer Dance" or "Song for Bringing a Child into the World." It should also be noted that in some cases I have made few changes in the original translations, while in others I have made more (always responsibly, I hope). Sometimes I have given these changes in the notes, but the reader can always check what I have done by referring to my sources.

I hope that after finishing this book readers will continue on to the volume I edited in 1995, *Coming to Light: Contemporary Translations of the Native Literatures of North America*, as well as to the books of translators represented there and to the books of those who aren't. This field is growing, and is exciting in the way it brings together Native and non-Native, academic study and actual singing and dancing. I hope too that the reader will regard this book as something of an incentive to attend a ceremonial or recreational event in Indian country, a Corn Dance at Cochiti, say, and the Powwow at Taos, both in July and both in New Mexico.[23]

To appreciate traditional Native American music and song one should simply *listen*. It is true that much Native American music is different from the music most of us are used to. It sounds different; it doesn't employ harmony and uses different techniques, scales, and rhythms. And it varies from tribe to tribe, region to region. Even with the best will, persons with ears trained in the Western mode have difficulty with it. Typical is the experience of the well-known conductor Leopold Stokowski, who visited Mabel Dodge Luhan at her house in Taos in the 1930s. Luhan, who had married Tony Luhan of Taos Pueblo, believed that in the Indian lay the salvation of the world. Stokowski was just the latest among those she tried to enlist in her cause. And he was more than willing. "With unwavering patience he spent night-long hours listening to the Indian songs and tried in vain to write down phrases, failing for lack of a scale. 'They are singing in thirty-seconds!' he whispered despairingly." Stokowski would have been better off simply listening, letting the music work its effect on a relaxed sensibility, freed of musical and cultural prejudices. Such a process should be easier today than it was earlier in the century. It took sickness to get Alice Fletcher to love the music after hearing it as "noise," "a screaming downward movement that was gashed by the vehemently beating drum." She underwent conversion during an illness when Francis La Flesche brought his family and friends to sing to her. Then, she reported, in this enforced period of passivity, "the sweetness, the beauty and the meaning of these songs were revealed to me."[24]

It has not been easy to find songs I could use. Frequently I'd come across lists of songs sung during ceremonies but with no attempt made to transcribe the songs themselves. Sometimes I'd find prose paraphrases or "this song cannot be translated," "meaning of song unknown," or "that which is given is only approximate." Not infrequently I came across something like this: "The words in part mean: Danger (?) (?) (?) I (?) (?) (?) my tracks."[25] But this is not surprising in view of the circumstances of collecting, the sacred nature of some of the songs, and the complexity of what "song" meant to the singer. For instance, when Knud Rasmussen asked the singer Heq what he meant by singing a song that nobody understood, neither its substance nor hints, he answered, "The spirit hymns have to do with supernatural and unreal things, so ordinary people do not need to understand them. The wisdom in them is often concealed and one must simply utter the words, which have a special power."[26]

Many songs are just the tip of an iceberg. The few enigmatic words need a body of myth or story to render them intelligible. Thus, "Where will I go in? / I will go in where green scum is on the pool" requires two pages of Yokuts myth to set the song in context and give it meaning.[27] A good number of songs use archaic or foreign words, or versions of a foreign tongue, often corrupted in the transition, their "otherness" showing "power." Some songs are intensely personal, attained during a spirit quest, with words allusive, illusive, cryptic, and to be used only on special occasions. Others are linked to dream and vision, are attained in dream and vision, the original singer being an animal or "object" who passes the song on. Such songs are "the medium of an inner journey."[28]

If there is any way of thinking of these versions as different from those made earlier in the century, I might suggest thinking of them not in assimilationist terms but in terms of "complementarity."[29] I would like to hope that they are part of the coexistence of "different modalities of reception and resistance."[30] My wish throughout has been to show the reader some of the immense variety and power of the originals, which range from the great Navajo Chantways to saucy, even ribald, songs of derision; from lullabies and children's songs to hunting songs and a song sung by an Inuit about the first airplane he ever saw. This volume is a gathering of samples from all over North America. I hope a certain inevitable flattening of effect produced by my individual voice is minimal. And clearly I could only use those songs that gave themselves to my largely lyric approach, to an aesthetic thoroughly "Western," even in its late romantic affinity for the non-Western, the non-familiar.[31]

As for the book's arrangement I have simply started in the north, in Alaska; moved south, through Canada, and wandered idiosyncratically down the Pacific Coast, and then east to the Plains and Eastern Woodlands, and then south; journeying finally over to California and the Southwest. There is no anthropology or ideology involved in this transit. The book just seemed to flow better that way.

In my notes I have identified where each selection comes from, and one or two times I have reproduced the original. I have also attempted to provide information so the reader can begin to see the work in its context. I venture to say that the songs can sometimes be understood outside the matrix of the notes, but a larger appreciation will entail reading song and note together.

Finally, I hope the reader will attend Indian ceremonies, where they are allowed to, and listen to Indian music, both live and recorded, traditional and "contemporary."[32] For the songs go on, they "stay alive and help our people survive," as the Osage scholar and poet Carter Revard notes.[33] Indian music is thriving, as are all the arts, particularly literature. The links between past and present are strong, despite everything, perhaps stronger now than at any time in this century. What the Hopi composer and musician Jacob Coin has said of music is true of all the arts: "Traditional music and contemporary music are extensions of each other."[34]

I would like to offer particular thanks to the laboratory of anthropology in Santa Fe for kindness and help in the research of this book while I was Visiting Fellow in 1994: Laura J. Holt, Librarian; Tracey Kimball, Assistant Librarian; Bruce Bernstein, Chief Curator and Assistant Director. I am grateful to Susan McGreevey (and Bro). Warm thanks also to Susan DiSesa, managing director of the Modern Library, and Ian Jackman, assistant editor at Random House: enthusiastic, supportive, and skillful editors and friends.

NOTES TO INTRODUCTION

1. For the historical and intellectual background, as well as the topic of translation, see my introduction to *Song of the Sky: Versions of Native American Song-Poems* (University of Massachusetts Press, 1993) and my introduction to a volume I edited in 1992, *On the Translation of Native American Literatures* (Smithsonian Institution Press). In the latter are two valuable essays on the subject of translation: Arnold Krupat's "On the Translation of Native American Song and Story" and William M. Clements' "'Tokens of Literary Faculty': Native American Literature in the Early Nineteenth Century." See also my introduction to *Coming to Light: Contemporary Translations of the Native Literatures of North America* (Random House, 1995).
2. Quoted in William M. Clements, "The Jesuit Foundations of Native North American Literary Studies," *American Indian Quarterly* 18, no. 1 (winter 1994), 51.
3. Washington Matthews, *Navajo Legends*, Memoirs of the American Folk-Lore Society, vol. 5 (1897); new edition, Foreword by Grace A. McNeley (University of Utah Press, 1994), 22.

4. On his first voyage, Columbus kidnapped some Natives to serve as interpreters, "that they might learn to speak." There was controversy at the time about whether the Natives were in fact human and hence capable of speech. But clearly Columbus must have heard them speaking, so theory and reality clashed; his phrasing is revelatory of that clash. As David Murray has pointed out, the idiom depends on an ideology of dominance and superiority, "on a set of assumptions about language and about civilization and its boundaries, according to which to speak a language which is utterly alien is the equivalent of speaking no language at all" (*Forked Tongues: Speech, Writing, and Representation in North American Indian Texts* [Indiana University Press, 1991], 6).

5. Willard Rhodes, "North American Indian Music: A Bibliographical Survey of Anthropological Theory," *Music Library Association Notes* 10 (1952), 33.

6. Nina De Shane, "Ethnomusicology and the Study of North American Indian Music," *Queen's Quarterly* 10, no. 1 (spring 1983).

7. Theodore Baker, *On the Music of the North American Indians*, trans. Ann Buckley (Fritz Knuf, 2707 Buren, The Netherlands, 1976; originally Leipzig, 1882).

8. Anonymous editorial, *The Etude: Presser's Musical Magazine*, special section on "Music of the American Indians," October 1920, 653.

9. Thurlow Lieurance, "The Musical Soul of the American Indian," *The Etude*, 655–656.

10. Ibid., 660.

11. Frederick R. Burton, *American Primitive Music: With Special Attention to the Songs of the Ojibways* (Kinnikat Press, Port Washington, N.Y., 1964), 188; originally published in 1909.

12. Ibid.

13. Ibid. Charles Skilton in the late 1930s thought the Indians had already developed musically as far as the moderns. He was attracted to Indian music, he said, because of the "many devices of the ultra-modern composers of the present day" that it employed, "such as unusual intervals, arbitrary scales, changing tune, conflicting rhythm, polychoral effects, hypnotic monotony" (quoted in *Beyond the Frontier*, ed. Paul Bohannan and Fred Plog [National History Press, New York, 1967], 340). Just what

Skilton meant by these terms is open to question. What "polychoral" effects had he heard, one wonders? The only groups ever documented whose style can be described as incorporating some polyphonic and contrapuntal effects live, according to Richard Keeling, in northern California (*Cry for Luck: Sacred Song and Speech Among the Yurok, Hupa, and Karok Indians of Northwestern California* [University of California Press, 1992]). For a good brief overview of the variety of Native American "musics" see Barbara Tedlock, "North American Indian Musics," in *Racial and Ethnic Directions in American Music* (Report of the College English Music Society, 1982), 9–27.

14. Fletcher was an assimilationist who had taken an active part in allotments, having been sent in 1883 to supervise the distribution of Omaha lands. She later did the same with the Winnebagos and Nez Perce. Her evolutionary ideas are clearly seen in her writings on Indian literature, where she talks about song structure that "reveals a groping after metrical form" and refers to "examples of nascent poetry" or the failure of "the sustained intellectual effort essential to the development of poetic art." See A *Study of Omaha Indian Music*, Archeological and Ethnological Papers of the Peabody Museum, vol. 1, no. 5 (1893), 247.

15. Both *Indian Action Songs* and *Indian Games and Dances* were published by C. C. Birchard and Co., Boston. No date was given for Fletcher's book, but I surmise about 1922. A blurb for these books from a University of Wisconsin professor says he'll use them in the twenty-one Chautauquas the university is "carrying on" that summer.

16. Natalie Curtis, *The Indians' Book*, Dover Books reprint, 1968, xxi.

17. Michael Castro, *Interpreting the Indian*, p. 11, quoting a Curtis article in the *American Review of Reviews*, 1907. This desire to infuse American art with what were regarded as the genuine impulses of Native American culture was common among intellectuals and artists of the early twentieth century. They promoted "Indian values" and used them to berate the positivist and materialist West. W. Jackson Rushing discusses this and related issues in *Native American Art and the New York Avant-Garde: A History of Cultural Primitivism* (University of Texas Press, 1995).

18. Jerome Rothenberg, *Shaking the Pumpkin: Traditional Poetry of*

the Indian North Americas, rev. ed. (Alfred van der Marck Editions, New York, 1985), xv.

19. Ibid., xvi.

20. Arnold Krupat, *Ethnocriticism: Ethnography, History, Literature* (University of California Press, 1992).

21. See Brian Swann, ed., *On the Translation of Native American Literatures*, 64–79. Rothenberg's "total translation" involves the creation of English vocables by "translating" the vocable sound in, say, Navajo. Thus, he translates *'eshkii* (boy) which might have the vocables *i* and *ye* added (*'eshikiyi*). This Rothenberg translates as "boyngnng" to convey the distortion in Navajo and link "boy" to the vocalic refrain. Unfortunately such instances can seem risible; in this case the effect is of a boy being struck and reverberating like a bell. William Bevis, in "American Indian Verse Translations" (in *Literature of the American Indians: Views and Interpretations*, ed. Abraham Chapman [New American Library, 1975], 308–323), takes Rothenberg to task and gives astringent critiques of Cronyn and Grove Day, as well as of William Brandon's *The Magic World: American Indian Songs and Poems* (William Morrow, 1971).

22. By "song-poem," a not particularly accurate phrase, I mean to include not only songs but recitative, prayer, and ceremony, a whole variety of Native American verbal and musical expression.

23. "Indian Country" is not just in the Western United States. Powwows are held all over, especially in summer, from Mashpee, Mass., and Oneida, Wis., to Richmond, Va., and even Queens, N.Y. For getting around Native America, the following article and books are very helpful: Don L. Roberts, "A Calendar of Eastern Pueblo Indian Ritual Drama," in Charlotte J. Frisbie, ed., *Southwestern Indian Ritual Drama* (University of New Mexico Press, 1980); Eagle/Walking Turtle, *Indian America: A Traveler's Companion* (John Muir Publications, Santa Fe, 1991); Ralph and Lisa Shanks, *The North American Indian Travel Guide* (Costano Books, Box 355, Petaluma, Calif. 94953, 1986). Two other books are also helpful: *The Reference Encyclopedia of the American Indian* (Todd Publications, 18 North Greenbush Road, West Nyack, N.Y. 10994) and Duane Champagne, ed., *The Native North American Almanac* (Gale Research, 1994).

24. The Stokowski incident is described in Marta Weigle and Kyle

Fiore, *Santa Fe and Taos: The Writers' Era, 1916–1941* (Ancient City Press, Santa Fe, 1982), 101; the Alice Fletcher incident is in Joan T. Mark, *A Stranger in Her Native Land: Alice Fletcher and the American Indians* (University of Nebraska Press, 1988), 221.

25. Julian H. Steward, "Ethnography of the Owens Valley Paiute," *University of California Publications in American Archeology and Ethnology* 33, no. 3 (1933). This is a Bear Shaman Song.

26. Knud J. Rasmussen, *Intellectual Culture of the Copper Eskimos,* trans. W. E. Calvert, *Report of the Fifth Thule Expedition, 1921–24,* vol. 9 (Copenhagen, 1932), 183.

27. James Hatch, *Tachi Yokuts Music,* Kroeber Anthropological Society Papers, no. 19 (fall 1958), 51. Vocables can be thought of as part of this "inner journey," as Richard Keeling hints (op. cit. note 13) when he notes, of a Hupa Deerskin Dance, that "in keeping with its sacred nature, the song is sung entirely in vocables" (p. 84). Vocables, until recently dubbed "meaningless syllables," can in fact be very complex. It has been pointed out, for example, that in Kwakiutl songs vocabalic introductions prefigured in microcosm the structure of the song as a whole, and David P. McAllester has said that the same thing can be seen in Navajo songs (*Hogans: Navajo Houses and House Songs* [Wesleyan University Press, 1980], 17).

28. Robin Ridington, "Beaver Dreaming and Singing," *Anthropologica* 13 (1978), 123.

29. The term is from Peter Mason, *Deconstructing America: Representations of the Other* (Routledge, New York and London, 1990), 159.

30. Ibid., 165.

31. On the question of native aesthetics, see Claire R. Farrer, "Aesthetics and Native North Americans," in Charlotte J. Frisbie, *Southwestern Indian Ritual Drama*; also David P. McAllester, *Enemy Way Music: A Study of Social and Esthetic Values as Seen in Navajo Music,* Papers of the Peabody Museum of American Archeology and Ethnology, 41 (1954). Rasmussen frequently discusses the topic in the volumes of the Fifth Thule Expedition, as does Tom Lowenstein in *Eskimo Poems from Canada and Greenland* (University of Pittsburgh Press, 1973).

32. Canyon Records and Indian House (Box 472, Taos, N.M. 87571)

are still the best publishers of Native American music; the latter specializes in traditional music, the former is more eclectic. SOAR (P.O. Box 8606, Albuquerque, N.M. 87198) is also a good source for traditional and contemporary music. The best place to discover what is going on in the native art world, including the world of music, is *Indian Artist* (544 South Guadalupe, Santa Fe, N.M. 87501).

33. Carter Revard, "Walking Among the Stars," in Brian Swann and Arnold Krupat, eds., *I Tell You Now: Autobiographical Essays by Native American Writers* (University of Nebraska Press, 1987), 79.

34. "A Hopi in Two Musical Worlds," exhibition catalog, Festival of American Folklife, Smithsonian Institution, 1992, 93. In the same catalog, pages 81–92, is an overview of the dynamic nature of Indian music by Thomas Vennum, Jr., "The Changing Soundscape in Indian Country."

WEARING THE MORNING STAR

SHAMAN'S SONG

The whale
the beluga
the hooded seal
the salmon
the caribou
the ground seal
the walrus
the polar bear
the fox
the bird
the wolf
the bone

SONG OF THE STONE

Men hear me

    jumping about

       with long leaps

  When the ice melts & there is lots of water

     I jump

       about

OLD SONG OF THE MUSK OX PEOPLE

It is glorious
when the caribou herds leave the forests
and begin to wander northward.
They are on the alert for deep pitfalls in the snow,
the great herds from the forests, when they spread out
                                    over the snow—
they are glorious.
It is glorious
when early summer's thin-coated caribou begin to wander.
When at Haningassoq, down there, over the promontories,
they mill back and forth looking for a crossing place.
It is glorious
when the great musk oxen
down there, glossy, black,
cluster in small groups
to face and watch the dogs.
When they bunch together like that
they are glorious!
The women down there are glorious
when they go visiting the houses in small flocks,
and the men down there suddenly feel
the need to boast and prove their manhood,
while the women try to catch them in a lie!
It is glorious
when the winter caribou with their thick coats
begin their trek back, in toward the forests.
They are glorious!
They look about anxiously for people.
When they are moving in toward the forests
they are glorious!
The enormous herds are glorious
when they begin to wander down there by the sea,

down by the beach.
The creaking whisper of hooves when they begin to wander
                                                around—

oh, it is glorious!

SONG OF THE SEA

Down there, that,
how shall I set foot on it,
the enormous new ice on the sea,
the one who croons anxiously like a mother to her young,
the one who raises its voice in song?
Listen—the one down there!
Shall I step on it,
the sea's enormous new ice down there,
the one who croons anxiously like a mother to her young,
the enormous new ice, that raises its voice in song?
Listen—the one down there!

The man gazes at it.

It follows you.

It has you in its thoughts.

AVUVNUK'S SONG

the great sea
                    has set me adrift
it moves me as the weed in a great river
        the earth and the weather
                                    move me
            they have carried me away
and transport my insides
                    with joy

SONG OF THE MUSK OX

It was the first time I'd ever seen them.
They were way off on the plain, in the distance,
far from the hill I was standing on.
Ignorant, I thought they were
small and puny.
So I ran as fast as I could,
and reached them out on the open plain—
but as I approached within range they grew up
from the ground, giant black beasts, the great musk ox
with glossy black hair.
And I shot some, far from any village,
in the lands of our happy summer hunting.

TWO SONGS OF DERISION

I

Here I am, I don't know why, except
I heard some things from Unganguaq
and I feel I have to pass them on—
how you two got it on together.
Yes, you, Utahania,
and your uncle Igjuk's younger sister,
Paningajaq, at Kidlinangaq,
just at the beginning of spring.
Yes, you two got it on together.
So, what did you say, dear kinswoman Paningajaq,
as you spread your legs nice and wide?
Was it hard when he stuck it in you?

II

I'm not much good at this sort of thing,
so I won't make this song too long.
He wanted his sister,
that's what people say.
He ought to be ashamed of himself!
Do you think I would make a pack of lies
into a song? Right—
he never cast longing looks
at his little sister. . . .
It's said that you, Utahania,
came creeping in to your little sister,
Qauatiovaq, with the intent
of fucking her. But when she said,
What do you want? you looked
rather foolish, didn't you?
And so, to show you for what you are,
I make this song.

THE WIDOW'S SONG

Why do people feel
no compassion for me?
Sleep comes hard
since Maula's killer
showed no mercy.

Is it so strange that I hurt
because I saw my only love
flung to the ground,
neck limp?
His enemies murdered him,
and maggots forever
prevented his homecoming.

And he was not the only one
to leave me. My small son
whom I loved
also raced to the land of shadows.

Now I'm like a beast
caught in the trap of my own house.

My journey on this earth will be long.
It is as if my footprints will always be stretching off into
                                        great distance.

A poor amulet is the only thing
I have left when
the northern lights dance their spark-play
                                       across the sky.

DELIGHT IN NATURE

Isn't it lovely,
the little river cutting through the gorge
when you approach it slowly
while trout are standing
behind stones in the stream?

Isn't it lovely,
the river's thick grass banks?
But I shall never again
meet Willow Twig, my dear friend
I long to see again.
Well, that's how it is.
The winding run
of the stream through the gorge
is lovely.

Isn't it lovely,
the bluish rocky island out there
when you approach it slowly?
What does it matter
that the blowing spirits of the air
stray over the rocks
because the island is lovely
when you approach it
at an easy pace
and haul it in?

SONG TO A MISER

I put together
words for a song,
a little song,
which I brought into the house one night,
unrecognizable, all swaddled up,
and threw under the sleeping-bench.

No one would share it,
no one could touch it
since it was mine alone,
mine mine mine,
secret and unshared!

SONG TO THE SPRING

I was far off in my kayak
keeping an eye out for land.

Here I came to a snowdrift
which had started to melt.

Then I knew it was spring
and we'd survived winter.

But I became afraid my eyes
would be too weak
to see all the lovely things.

PTARMIGAN

A small ptarmigan sat
in the middle of the plain
on top of a snowdrift.
Its eyelids were red
and its back streaked brown.
And right under its cute tail feathers—
the sweetest little rump.

LOVEMAKING

My playmate
strokes me across my belly,
takes me, gives
her body, tears
the skin bracelets
from my wrists.

[Little Daughter dances and sings]

It's about time I challenged you,
cousin, to a song duel!
My anger is waking!
I was out fetching fire—
domestic as always—
when, in your stupid vanity,
you started showing off
to my stepfather.
Do I lie, or am I telling the truth?
Come now and test me
while my anger is growing.

[Pearl jumps up, dances, and sings]

Come over here to my side,
you who will defend me.
Take the lamp's wick,
dip it in seal oil, light it.
Let the light fall
on Little Daughter's face.
Listen, cousin—
am I lying, or am I telling the truth?—
once I surprised you
doing it with Asarpana!
Make fun of her,
you who are on my side.
Grab her, friends,
and throw her to the ground.
Do you still think, cousin,
you can measure up to me?
Let's make fists and fight!
Let's race,
the loser to hand over her man!

[Now Pearl jumps up again and dances to the front, singing a
song designed to make the audience laugh]

Well, let me be
a little naughty, just
a little naughty:
If there was somebody
who'd just stroke
or even touch
my belly, then I wouldn't
be so angry or fret
because another woman
was ogling my man!

[Little Daughter]

I get jealous easily
and am angry fast.
Here I am, standing,
forgetting my poor songs.
But listen up, cousin,
you who want so much
to mock me in song—
Let's go visit
the people at the shore.
There I'll answer
your clumsy song of spite!

[Now all get up and go to the village on the shore. On the way, Pearl sings]

I'll attack the people on the shore,
I'll take your friends away from you.
I'll expose you girls
for what you are:
all smiles on the outside
but shameless underneath.
You embrace men willingly,
without a thought, then
later, in secret, give birth
in the mountains.
Am I lying, or am I telling the truth?
I often envied those people
who slept innocently at night:

virtuous people don't see anything.
Yet even they say
you've given birth in secret.
Do I lie, or am I telling the truth?

[Here Little Daughter starts crying. Now Pearl has an idea]

Let's go singing
and visit the people at the shore.
We'll open Little Daughter's sewing box,
rummage around, and
bring into the open
all her pitiful sweet little secrets!
Hey, friends, grab her!

[They grab her and hold her tight while Pearl continues singing]

This festive time brings us all together!
Grab her round the belly,
rock her hips!

[And now they force Little Daughter to dance while Pearl sings]

Showing no mercy,
we'll reveal her hidden thoughts,
she who always fished for
the man I love! *Now*
my anger is coming,
cousin!

[They reach the village, but here Pearl's husband unexpectedly
leaps forward into the circle and sings]

Now *my* anger is waking too!
Do you hear, do you hear?
I'm spoiling for a fight!
Do you hear, do you hear?
Let's break into the house
and smash all the piss pots,
tear up the membrane windows,
toss the lamp on the dunghill
and do the same with the meat!
Destroy, destroy the racks

for skins and food!
I'm really in the mood for a fight!
I'm boiling with rage,
hot for song, for song!

Look at that wretched girl there.
I often had fun with her.
Oh, we were like beasts in heat
when we went for a walk in the mountains.
Oh, I remember when we went
to Great Lichen Mountain—
favorite tumbling ground
for male animals!
Wagging our tails, we looked out
over the light-drenched lands
to the south, then
threw ourselves down in the heather.

But what's happening now?
Nobody answers? Well,
keep your mouths shut.
We'll go home and you can rest.
Dawn's light is approaching
over the mountain. Dawn
has replaced night.

TO HELP MAKE THE AFTERBIRTH COME OUT

What is this?
The afterbirth?
Come and be set out for blowflies.
What is this?
Come and be set out for bees.
You who usually come loose at the outer edges,
it is chilly inside there, it is chilly.

THE SONG OF AMATOQ

While I stood alone at the breathing hole,
    longing for women,
missing my friends, or rather
    their women, just then
they swam past me below
    and out to the ocean, out there.

It was early afternoon
    when I walked into camp
with my friend Inugtigjuaq,
    who has dark face hair;
I who have no children to come out
    running to meet me, just
an old dog, nothing else.

    While I was yearning for women
I found the trail of a caribou calf,
    a little calf, nothing more,
there, where cows with young grazed.
    I was annoyed.
I came upon it from behind

and it was unafraid,
and I didn't give it the bearded seal's skin
    to make into thongs,
and I didn't give it
    the polar bear's skin.
Yes, it was I.

IT IS HARD TO CATCH TROUT

This song I want to use,
this song I wish to put together,
I wonder why it will not come to me?
At Sioraq, at a fishing hole in the ice,
I could feel a little trout on the line,
and then it was gone.
I stood jiggling the line.
Why is it so difficult?
When summer came, and the waters opened up,
fishing became really hard.
I'm just no good at it.

NETSILIK DRUM DANCES

I: Siutinuaq's Song

How shall I make this song?

How shall I use it?

This song has an important meaning.

I just remembered them,
I just remembered them.

Caribou going toward the mountain.
It's winter there.
The distance is very great.

I am just recalling them.

Who reminded you?

He did not pull the bowstring back.
He was creeping uphill toward it.
He might have caught it.

I just remembered them.
I just remembered them.

It was close to Nuarliqangaqjuq and Lake Tasiqjuq.
He walked in the wet snow
toward the mainland,
to the place where people live,
a joyful place.
He didn't think he could do it.
It was summer down there.

Here spring drags on so long.
He remembered he was afraid.

II: Luke Uqualla's Song

I am learning this song.
I made it.

I caught a fish in the morning, down there.
In spring, just sitting at the edge of the sand
makes you want to make happy sounds.

I was not so happy, however.

Later, looking out of the miserable tent I always look
out of,
I caught sight of a caribou with her yearling.
I needed them, so, not thinking clearly,
I took off after them running.

I didn't catch up until we'd reached the edge
of the sea.
They fell at low tide.

Now I will use them for future springs and summers
to help me on my way.

In spring, above the place where I had been walking,
I fell asleep. When I woke,
I began to walk
on the sandy soil
of Qimirjuk, over there.

III: Arnaluaq's Song

I am learning this song,
I'm working on it.
How will I be able to sing it in the dance house?
I really want to sing it there.
I will learn it.

But maybe I'll forget it.

Yes! Yes! I have it—
but it's not perfect.
I'm only singing it.
I will really learn it because
I want to sing it in the dance house.
I will learn it.

But maybe I'll forget it.

It worries me.

I am anxious in spring
when the people always
travel to the hunting grounds,
to places where no one lives.

I really wanted to see
caribou shedding their old coats.
I moved to a higher place
and faced the winter hunting grounds,
the place where there were no people.
I really wanted to see
a fat seal
waiting to be caught
on top of the thick ice.
I really wanted to see
caribou shedding old coats,
waiting to be caught.

I was looking for them.
I climbed to the hilltop to look about
at the land all around me:
the place where skins are dried,
the caribou crossing,
down there, the fish-drying place.
Everywhere was empty.

You could see the landmarks like grease stains:
Qadlutiag Bay,
the shelf on the cliff where the birds nest,
much closer to the big hill.

I was looking all around for game.
I decided to lie down
on the leeward side of the hunting place.
I thought I would never hear or see anything.
But something came splashing out of the water.

It was only a little ptarmigan on top of the snow.
But I chased it as if it was
a fat seal or a precious skin.

Later, I was able to get
a good fish, a small fish but good.
I hurried home as if it was
a seal, or something with a lot of meat.

IV: Qayutinuaq's Song

Up there, up there
I was usually silent
inside my little house.
I was usually silent up there.

Then, it appeared.
One morning, it appeared up there.

Up there,
let me make songs with it in my little house.
Let me make songs with it up there.

Up there
I was usually silent.
Inside my little house
I was usually silent
up there.

V: Quuksun's Song

How shall I make this one?

The song might not come out well,
though I can certainly do it.
I can finish it for everyone.

How shall I make it?
It might not come out well.

My wife is so lovable,
but the neighbors don't like her.
I am tired of looking away, up at the sky,
pretending they aren't talking.
I like to support you, my wife.

I feel lonely when I am outside
our village. I have no one
to make me feel good.

I tried to find
all the animals you wanted.
I called all the spirits.
It's a hard thing to do.

I feel frustrated
in summer
walking on the mainland.
I am not going to find anything.

I usually walk on the sea ice in winter,
looking for seals.
I won't be able to
sing up a seal.

But I can do it.
I'm just pretending.

I called out for the spirits

of the fishes
in the breathing holes.
I called out for the spirits.
I have been waiting and watching.

Because I can catch something
I called out for the spirits.

I have not seen them
all winter.
I have not seen them.

VI: Iqquqaqtuk's Song:
What will this turn out to be?

When I hear a sound I
always turn around.

When I saw this
it was gliding.

It started circling
and began to descend.
It was coming straight at me
with the nose pointed down.

When it got near the ground
it settled down, leveled off.
As it touched the ground
it jumped up and down.

I'll always remember it clearly,
the airplane, that winter.

When it started moving again
it made an awful noise.
The tail started wagging back and forth,
shaking hard,
bouncing up and down.

The tail was wagging.

I wouldn't be able to follow it
to the land of its people.
I often remember that.
I couldn't do it.

I started jumping up and down
like it, on top of the hills.
I jumped as if I had spotted an animal
fit for food.
I was jumping up and down
because of that great buzzing noise.

I never thought I would be afraid
and run away from game.
But I was afraid, and ran.
I, who whip in my dogs in the fall,
ran away from that terrible noise.

SONGS FROM ESKIMO POINT

No. 10

I recall something.
I recall the words of a stranger
                        about forever.

A person came down from the sky,
                telling them not to be afraid;
                        they would be hearing
                        about life, spiritual life, soul.
        A baby will be born.

No. 16

How am I going to sing? The lead dog
        just gets angry in the deep snow.

In the deep snow I have to run
        to follow the tracks.

I want to get closer to you.

INUPIAT DANCE SONGS

I
I lost at checkers.
You made this song.
Now I make my move,
inventing the dance to it.

Here, under the ice ridge,
dance hunkered down real low and
make farting noises.

II
People inside themselves feel warm.
Try to see a bright light.
Don't be afraid of anything
while waiting.

III
They'd plunged through bauchy snow,
        and now these bearded men,
home after hunting the whale,
        are dancing in a circle
which their uncle will run out
        and join, happy, proud.

IV

The sun shines over the point.
The point shines, also moving.
I am going to pile rocks on top of brown bear,
polar bear. Here the land beckons me:
brant goose, sandhill crane.

What is that hanging down in the middle of your window?
Your granny's honey bucket. Lick it. Kiss it.
Point Barrow people are dogs,
their only drinking water salt.

TEASING SONGS

I
Ruti, the old lady with
    the pretty trimmed boots,
is emptying her slop bucket.

II
Give me my fur pants.
    I want to get the lice out.
They are so big
    you have to hit them with a hammer.

LOVE SONG I

My breath
> is here
My bones
> are here
My flesh
> is here

I seek you with them
I find you with them

> Speak to me
> Say something to me

THE OLD MAN

She is about to appear in the doorway, there, in the doorway!

She came and shed her light on me.
> But
>> I took off again, inland, not knowing which way
>>> to walk, not knowing how to get past that house
> down there by the shore—
>>>> I reacted as any sensible man
>>> would have reacted—
>>>>> I let myself be scared off
>> by him,
>>> that old man with the bitter mouth.

LOVE SONG II

Not enough
                never enough of her
     that one   dancing there   dancing
never enough
               of the smell of her body
        wafting
   to me
never enough

I cannot live without her breath

LOVE SONG OF WARNING

I tell him, Don't go to her.
You go to her, my darling,
I'll stick a knife in your ribs.
Leave me before I give the say-so,
I'll also stick your friends.

GREAT BLUE HERON CHILDREN'S SONG

The great blue heron stands in the shallow water
                                    near the shore.
The great blue heron spears clams and
                skips them along the water
                            toward the beach.

LITTLE BOY'S MOURNING SONG

Mother in the ocean
did not see the big wave.
Now she is lost in the kelp.

Fart, fart,
fart—the billy goat has eaten
too much soup.

I paddle far out, fast, to avoid
being done in by its fury,
and tie a cloth around my head.

TWO POTLATCH SONGS

I

"Do not look around, people, do not look around, or
    we might see something that will hurt us in the great
                        chief's great house.
Do not look around, do not look around, or else we might see
    something frightful in the great chief's great house,
the house in which Tsonoqoa lives. Therefore we are paralyzed
    and cannot move. The house of our war chief,
                         our potlatch chief,
is taking our breath and our lives.
    Make no noise, people, make no noise, or we'll start
an avalanche of wealth from our chief, the
                      overhanging mountain."

"I, Neqapenkem, am he from whom the red cedar bark
                      comes down,
    from whom it is untied for the chiefs of the tribes.
Do not complain, you people, in the house of the great chief
    at whose hands all are afraid to die, over whose body
is sprinkled the blood of those who try to eat
    in the house of the chief, the great chief.
One thing only makes me mad: when people eat little
    of the food provided by the great chief, and eat it slowly."

II

Is someone else causing this smoky weather? No, I, Henakalaso,
    am the only one on earth, the only one in the world
                      who makes
thick smoke rise for my guests from the beginning
                      of the year to
    its end. What will my rival say again, that spider woman?
What will he pretend to do next? That spider woman's words

do not take a straight path. Will he not brag that he is
going to break coppers, going to give a grease feast?
    That's what he'll say, that spider woman, and
                                        because of that
your faces are dry and moldy, you who are standing
    in front of your chief's belly. Nothing will satisfy you,
Neqapenkem. But sometimes I treated you so roughly
    you begged for mercy. Do you know what my mercy
will be like now? I will treat you like an old bitch,
    and you will spread your legs before me
                                    when I get aroused,
just like you did when I broke the great coppers
    "Cloud" and "Making Ashamed," and
                                    the other great coppers
"Chief" and "Killer Whale," and the one named
    "Point of the Island," and "Feared One" and "Beaver."
I throw this in your face, you I have always tried to vanquish,
    whom I have mistreated; you who dare not stand up
when I am eating, you, the chief whom even weaklings
                                            try to best.
    Now, my feast! Go to him, the impoverished creature
who wants to be fed by the chief whose name is
                                    "Full of Smoke,
    The Greatest Smoke." Then leave him alone,
                                    but give him
plenty to eat and make him drink till his stomach
    turns, and he vomits.
My feast steps over the fire, right up to the chief.

SONG OF A LOVER

        I wish his legs were broken
        so he couldn't follow you,
            my love.
        I wish your husband
        was blind so he couldn't

                    watch you,
                      my love.

                 Don't slap him,
             don't punch him in the face,
                      my love,
                 Copper-Maker-Woman,
         Copper-Made-to-Come-to-the-House-
                      Woman,
            Snare-Making-Woman, Chief Woman,
                      my love.

LOVE SONG OF A MAN
SENT TO HUNT GOATS
TO GET TALLOW FOR HIS BELOVED

You are cruel.
My tears run down as a stream.
into the middle of my room
because of you.
My tears are like a flood
because of you.
At that place in the rocks where they slope away,
where they slope away from me, here and there,
I slip down again and again when I climb
because of you,
my love.

LOVE SONG

The pain is terrible.
The pain is in all the wrong places.
It is on each side of my neck
so I cannot turn around for you.
The pain is in each eye
so I can't turn to look at you.
The pain is in my front teeth
so I cannot eat,
my love.

A BOY'S SONG

"Baby! Big baby!"
they call me when I play with them.
They taunt me:
"Baby! Big baby!"
What do they call me when I tease the little girls,
when I stick my finger up their vaginas,
when I throw stones at the other kids?
"Baby! Big baby!"

LOVE SONG

To me, your love is the pain of fire
traveling downward,
the pain
moving down.
To me, your love is a sickness.
It is like a body all boils, on fire.

I am thinking of the words you spoke,
I am thinking of you, your love for me.

I am afraid of your love.

Where is she going?
She will be taken far away, and leave me.
My body is numb because of what I said.

Good-bye, my love.

CARIBOU MEDICINE SONGS

I

Caribou doe,
bring your calves.
Bring them slowly to feed
on the land here where you will find plenty.
When you come,
come carefully.
My patient's spirit hovers nearby.
Don't crowd in with your calves
in case you trample his spirit.
As you draw near
his health will return.

II

Caribou,
I need your help.
You see I have laid my hands
on the sufferer.
Come and place your hooves where
I have laid my hands.
I need your help.
Without your help
there is no healing in my hands today.
Come here so quick
your tail stands erect.

SHAMING SONG FOR BUSHY-SNATCH

Mistelos stole too much.
Along with my wife, he took my child.

Put a brave face on, all you mothers, as I tell the world
of your ugliness:
You'll have a tough time now your tits
have dropped to your waist
and swing about.

SHAMAN SONG

It waved up and down,
the sky waved up and down when they
sang of salmon.

They placed eagle down
on the water in the bowl
where I was.
Then Anunitsektnim
pulled me out.

I gazed upon
the source of my power
when it stood up
in the center
of a place
of petrified power.

MAN'S LOVE SONG I

If you went to the sky
    I'd become a star
and catch you.
If you went to the ocean
    I'd become a bullhead
and catch you.

MAN'S LOVE SONG II

If you went to the land
of the bullhead
I'd become a kingfisher.
I'd dive down and
eat you.

WILD WOMAN'S SONG

> That otter
> was just swimming
> into the basket trap,
> had just entered the trap,
> just coming in—
>
> when I hit him with my clitoris
> and killed him stone dead!

BEAR'S SONG

> that sky
> I can feel
> with my paws
> to the sky
> I can reach right

BEAVER'S SONG

I build dams,
I build dams.
I build and watch
the water lilies grow.

CHINOOK SONGS

I
Kitty Apples is very unhappy
        this winter.
   Who will take her away?
     The steamboat Hope.

II
What is Billy doing now?
     He is going to the beer house.

The American says, *Get out of my way!*
     Billy leaves, crying.

OJIBWE CRADLE SONG

Who is this,
who is this
with wide bright eyes
at the top of my lodge?

It is I,
the little owl,
it is I,
the little owl,
coming
down,
it is I,
swooping
down . . .

*Look out, baby,
look out!*

CARIBOU HUNTING SONG

When I hunt caribou
    I feel as if they are standing still
        even if they are running away from me
    I feel as if they are standing still

How easy it is when I go to kill caribou

TRAPPING SONG

The animal says
        Is this where we will play?
        Is this where you are playing?

SONG FOR THE MUSKRAT

This is the hole which is the home
    of the muskrat

I am going to live
    with the muskrat

ARAPAHO GHOST DANCE SONGS

I

How bright the moonlight
how bright the moonlight
as I ride in with my load of buffalo meat

II

My father did not recognize me.
Next time he saw me he said,
You are the child of a crow.

III

I am looking at my father

I am looking at him

     he is beginning to turn into a bird

        turning into a bird

IV

They say
the spirit army is approaching,
the spirit army is approaching,
the whole world is moving onward,
the whole world is moving onward.
See, everybody is standing, watching.
Everybody is standing, watching.

V

The whole world is coming,
a nation is coming, a nation is coming.
The Eagle has brought the message to the people.
The father says so, the father says so.
Over the whole earth they are coming.
The buffalo are coming, the buffalo are coming.
The Crow has brought the message to the people,
the father says so, the father says so.

VI

My children, my children,
it is I who wear the morning star on my head.
It is I who wear the morning star on my head.
I show it to my children.
I show it to my children.

PAIUTE GHOST DANCE SONG

             Snowy earth
comes
         swirling
    ahead
       of the whirlwind
          ahead
                of the whirlwind
             snowy earth
                      swirling

WOLF LULLABY

I was running along the hillside when
    I fell and skinned my knee.

In the distance I saw a wolf,
    the redheaded one.

His face itched. No matter how hard
    he scratched he couldn't get at it.

He kills in all seasons.
    His face gets yellow with fat.

SONGS OF DERISION

I

White-on-the-side-of-the-neck,
    I'll slip my cunt over your neck
        and send you on your way.

Bob-tail Wolf,
    I'll stick you up my ass and walk about.
      When you're good and stinky
          I'll let you out.

II: Gray Bull's Song

Medicine-doll Woman,
       you can't dance,
           you claim you own a gun sheath
               but all I see are your balls
                   hanging down to your knees.

THE YELLOW STAR

The yellow star has noticed me.
It has given me a yellow feather,

that yellow star.

THE WHITE FOX

It comes from afar.
Earth's expanse is wide.
My brother the fox spoke, and said:
Look up and see the earth's expanse.
The foxes know the earth is wide.

SONG OF THE DEER SOCIETY

Spring is opening up.
I can smell the different perfumes
of the white weeds used in the dance.

PAWNEE LOVE SONG

Even worms
love each other,
so why not
us?

SONGS OF THE AWARI
OR GROUND-BREAKING CEREMONY

I
Now the land is cleared

II
the black earth you
distribute and scatter,
the ground of black being
you rouse,
Evening Star

III
now soil slips sideways,
mother earth comes sideways

IV
earth is coming,
life's vigor is coming

V
now you aim,
you aim at the earth

VI
you aim where women
are putting into the earth
my mother, life's vigor,
mother corn

VII
now it is budding,
the earth is budding

sprouts peep out,
the earth is calling

VIII
earth,
you are looking at it,
here it is, mother,
here it is, earth-
energy that infuses,
here it is,
my mother

IX
earth
they are scattering,
tossing about from the
coiled gambling basket—
see those two tossing it about,
they are scattering life,
those two are tossing it about,
life's force

TWO NEWE SONGS

I

   Song Woman
sits beating the rhythm of her song.
   Song Woman
sits beating the rhythm of her song
there in a distant place,
next to her cousin, the water,
beating the rhythm of her song,
beating the rhythm of her song.

II

There, in a distant place, she sits in an arroyo.
There, in a distant place, she sits in an arroyo
            winnowing the pine nuts,
      by the red-rock-wooded place
            winnowing the pine nuts.

THE RED WAGON'S DUST

red
wagon
dust
white man
looking around

RECITATIVE OF THE MOUNTAIN BLUE JAYS

Panther, it's too bad you took off
since I was planning to make
a panther-skin blanket of you.
It's too bad you had to retreat.
I can see you there in the distance,
heading for the mountains.
What's so important in the mountains?
It's too bad you keep talking to yourself,
you I intend to kill.

Wolf, you say you have great power.
Too bad your flesh will soon be
the earth on which it's lying.

MUSCOGEAN CHARM SONG

The fish pulled themselves
out of the stream.

One man pushed another
off a high cliff.
He said:
Fish in the stream!

TO GO TO THE WATER

Now
you have come to listen,
Long Person,
you are staying right here,
Helper of Humans,
you never relax your grip,
you never let go your grip on the soul.
You have taken a firm hold on the soul.
I originated at the cataract, not so far away.
I will stretch out my hand to where you are.
My soul has come to bathe in your body.
The white foam will cling to my head
as I go on with my life,
the white staff will come into my outstretched hand.
The fire in the hearth will be left burning for me.
The soul has been raised gradually to the seventh upper world.

CREEK DRUNKEN DANCE

I don't know a thing. I'm drunk.
We're drinking great stuff—
great, right?

Let's go, she says to me,
I've got no husband.
Your bed—where is it?
Tell me the way to your house.
My husband's asleep,
I'll run away from him,
I'll take off.
He's at home.
I'll run away.

My wife's home too, I say.
I'll run away too.
When the moon rises
I'll screw you, right here,
right up the middle of your belly,
I'll take up all your insides.
I'll screw you, I'll
sleep with you just
one night—
the road's close by—
just four nights
in that old house—
just ten nights
I'll sleep with you—

"Her husband will whip her,
and beat you up."

WARPATH SONG

I ran to the brook to do my hair.
I painted my face with colors of the evening skies.
My aunt chose a bright blue shawl for me, blue as the sky.
But then we heard the cry that meant
darkness to all my people.

I ran back to my tent.
I washed off all the paint
with my tears.

LULLABY

A baby's on the way.
She's swimming in the water
like a little rabbit.
She's got little rabbit feet.

COMANCHE PEYOTE SONGS

Dawn is breaking. He is carrying water this way.

Dawn rays are hanging down. Get up! The sun has risen!

Rooster.

Duck comes down.

Are you on your feet?

Daylight is coming.

Jesus have mercy on us, come down!

It has a red flower, it has power.

Daylight, red flower.

It moves along.

Yellow rays, dawn rays are standing up.

Power is flying.

Bird.

It is daylight. Get up!

The day came seven times. It is Sunday.

Dawn is coming. Wake up!

Morning is flying across. Get up!

It is coming.

It is surely coming.

It is hanging still.

The red bloom is standing toward the sun.

Haul the tipi poles.

Why are you hiding from me? The wind is coming.

The wind is coming. Run to the creek.

From the south it is coming.

Day is coming.

I am bringing dawn. You are coming from the east.

What are you bringing? I am bringing peyote.

An old woman is standing.

I got lost. My pipe, my hatchet. . . .

Go out, it is dawn. The eagle.

Get up, it is day. The sun rises. The smoky fog rises.

Day is coming. Cane brace.

Let me sing that song.

Across from the east.

It is from the south.

The wooden object flew up.

It will come. The sun moves.

From the east it stands still; at the creek a tree stands.

Get up, get up, it is daylight! Get up!

Tekwakï is praying. Eagle! Arise!

Looking back gladly.

People, arise.

It is dawn. Are you at the creek?

It is dawn. Look over there.

Reed whistle.

It is shaking its horns.

Yellow bloom; name it.

He is standing, the wind is blowing.

Coming down slowly.

The sun is coming.

Wings beating.

It is dawn. You must stand up.

A person is there; peyote is good.

A horse is coming down.

Move into line, it is daybreak.

Male antelopes, breeding.

A bird is circling, crying out.

A bird is getting ready to fly.

Beaver, it is dawn.

Dawn is coming. Blaze up the fire!

It is dawn.

Hide, the wind is blowing.

What are you holding? A dove?

Four turkeys grazing along.

Old woman standing.

Rise! We shall, when Jesus comes down.

Dawn is coming. Over the hill.

Coyote, coming down.

FROM THE SENDING

The Puma

It has been said that,
at that time and place, in this house,
the Honga, a people who possess seven fireplaces,
spoke to the one who had made his body of the Puma,
saying: O grandfather,
we have nothing that is fit for use as a symbol.
The Puma replied quickly: Little ones,
you say you have nothing for use as a symbol,
but I am one who is fitted for use as a symbol.
Look at the male puma, lying on the earth.
I am the one who has made his body of the male puma.
The knowledge of my courage has spread over the land.
Look at the god of day, who sits in the heavens.
I am a person who sits close to the god of day.
When the little ones make their bodies of me
they shall always be free from all causes of death
as they travel life's path.

Look at the great red boulder that sits on the earth.
I am the person who draws to himself the power
                                           of that boulder.
Even the gods themselves stumble
over me as I sit immovable.
When the little ones make their bodies of me
even the gods will trip over them, and fall.
Even the great gods themselves
as they move over the earth pass around me
as I sit immovable as the great red boulder.
When the little ones make their bodies of me
even the gods themselves shall pass around them
in forked lines as they travel life's path.
Even the great gods themselves

are afraid to stare at me insolently.
When the little ones make their bodies of me
even the gods will be afraid
to stare them in the face as they travel life's path.

It has been said, at that time and place,
in this house, he said to them: Behold,
the Black Bear, without blemish, that lies on the earth.
I am a person who has made his body of the Black Bear.
See the god of night who sits in the heavens.
I am the person who makes the Black Bear
                              draw his power from the god of night.
Regard the great black boulder that sits on the earth.
I am a person who sits next to the great black boulder.
Regard the great black boulder that sits on the earth.
When the little ones make their bodies of
                              the great black boulder
even the great gods themselves
shall stumble over them and fall.
Even the gods themselves
as they move over the earth pass around me in forked lines
                    as I sit immovable as the great black boulder.
When the little ones make their bodies of me
even the gods themselves
shall pass around them in forked lines as they travel
                                        the path of life.

Truly, at that time and place, in this house, it has been said
that he said to them: Regard the great white swan.
I am a person who has made his body of the great white swan.
Look at the god of night, the Male Star, the Morning Star.
I am a person who has made his body of the god of night.
Regard the great white boulder that sits on the earth.
I am a person who has made his body of
                              the great white boulder.
When the little ones make their bodies of me
even the gods themselves
shall stumble over them and fall.
Even the gods themselves

as they move over the earth pass around me as I sit immovable
                              as the great white boulder.
When the little ones make their bodies of me
even the gods themselves
shall pass around them as they pass around
                              the great white boulder.

At that time and place, in this house, it has been said
that he said to them: Behold the bull elk who sits on the earth.
I am the person who makes the bull elk draw his power
                              from the yellow boulder.

Behold the Female Star, the evening star.
I am the person who makes the yellow boulder draw its power
                              from the evening star.
When the little ones make their bodies of me
even the gods themselves
shall stumble over them and fall.
Even the gods themselves
as they move over the earth pass around me
                as I sit immovable as the great yellow boulder.
When the little ones make their bodies of me
even the gods themselves
shall pass around them as they pass around
                              the great yellow boulder.
Even the gods themselves
are afraid to bite me in anger.
When the little ones make their bodies of me
the gods themselves will be afraid to bite them in anger.

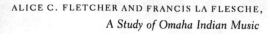

WOLF SONG

The women they
have gone out for firewood.
They are happy, walking together.

Here
I am walking,
wretched, uphappy.

WAGANCA'S SONG

I have let my love for you be known.
 Last night, when you called out,
your name came unbidden to my lips.
 When they asked, Who is that moving about
        in the shadows?
I blurted out *Waganca*!
 And so gave myself away.

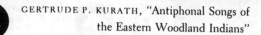

IROQUOIS TROTTING DANCE SONG

>   Little woman
>   I gave her a drink
> two glasses
>   she's already
>   smiling

THE DESERTED WOMAN

I can still just make them out   *going away*

There she was left   on a little islet

She began   to pick gooseberries

WOMAN'S SONG

It must have been hot
real hot
where you've just come from
because your balls
are
hanging
so

WINTU DREAM DANCE SONGS

I

                                        we shall go
                              along the flowery path
                        above we shall go
              along the Milky Way we shall go
Above we shall go

II

                                        Above
                              where the minnow
                  sleeps, at rest,
              the flowers
          droop

                              again
                        rise
              flowers
          The

III

We ghosts dance
down west,
down west.
Down west is where
we weeping ghosts dance,
where we ghosts dance.

IV

                                    swaying
                                rhythmically
                              dandelion puffs
                          rhythmically swaying
                          the ghosts of people
                        is where they will go
                        above I have heard
                    rhythmically swaying
                  the ghosts of people
                is where they will go
          I have heard
Above

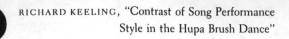

HUPA LOVE SONG

where we used to make love
　　　　　now
the grass is grown up high

COYOTE'S SONG

Coyote said: What am I?
    I am Coyote!
Coyote said: Who am I?
    I am Coyote!

SONG OF THE ECLIPSE

Leave me with a little sun.
    Don't eat it all.
    Leave me just
      a little.

YOKUTS PRAYER

Look at me!
Look at me:

        Tüüshiut,
        Yuhahait,
        Echepat,
        Pitsuriut,
        Tsukit,
        Ukat!

All of you, help me.
My words are tied in
with the great mountains,
    the great rocks,
    the great trees;
tied in with
my body and my heart.
All of you, help me
with your powers.
You too, day
and night.
All of you see me
one with this world.

LUISEÑO SONGS OF THE SEASONS

I

The ant has his season;
he has opened his house.
When the days grow warm he comes out.
The spider has her house and her hill.
The butterfly has her enclosure.
The chipmunk and squirrel have their hollowed logs for acorns.
It is time for the eagle to take off.
It will soon be time for the acorns to fall from the trees.

II

In the north the bison have their breeding grounds,
and the elk drops her young.
In the east the mountain sheep
and the horned toad have their young.
In the south other animals give birth.
In the west the ocean is heaving,
tossing its waves back and forth.
Here, at this place, the deer sheds his hair
and the acorns grow fat.
The sky sheds, changing color,
white clouds swept away.

III

    The Milky Way lies stretched out on its back,
making a humming sound.

    From the door of my house I recognize in the distance
Nahut, the stick used to beat Coyote, and Kashlapish,
      the ringing stones. I look up.

Look: Antares is rising,
      Altair is rising. The Milky Way,
         Venus is rising.

SENYAM PLANTING SONG

A wild goose landed on the heart's core.
    A little white seagull landed on the heart's core.
A wild goose landed on the heart's core.
    A little white seagull landed on the heart's core.
            So we stayed.
A wild goose landed on the heart's core.
    A little white seagull landed on the heart's core.
        Plants sprouted and burst into bloom.
A small bee landed on the heart's core.
  A larger bee landed on the heart's core.

THE EAGLE CEREMONY

He is hopping about, ready to lift off into air,
     my eagle, my eagle.

        Calling, he is gone,
          black eagle.
        The white eagle nests
          on high cliffs.
        The eagle from the west
          nests in sycamores
        along creeks.

      The egrets are screaming up in the nest.
      The chicken hawk is there too.

In the sky, the sun has set.
        Orion is emerging.
        The Pleiades are rising.

      The waves say: I am beating back and forth.
         The water rolls,
         the water rolls.
      The eagle says: I am here
         at the edge of the surf.

      Look, the eagle is swooping down,
          the eagle is flying,
       look.
          My eagle is
              colored red.

Coming, the eagle is black.
　　Going, the eagle is black.
Your eagle is white
　　going to the water.
My black eagle is coming.

My eyes are flowing with tears.

　　Done.
　　It is done.

SONG OF THE SKY LOOM

Mother Earth   Father Sky
                    we are your children

        With tired backs we bring you gifts you love

        Then weave for us a garment of brightness,
             its warp the white light of morning,
                weft the red light of evening,
                   fringes the falling rain,
                its border the standing rainbow.

        Thus weave for us a garment of brightness
        so we may walk fittingly where birds sing,
        so we may walk fittingly where grass is green.

Mother Earth   Father Sky

SAN JUAN BASKET DANCE

Prelude Dance
At a place on the mountaintop where we gather evergreen
                                                    boughs
    the Rain God Youths are singing beautifully.
At a place on the mountaintop where we gather
                                        evergreen boughs
    the Spruce Maidens are singing softly.
The sacred evergreen is right here at earth-navel,
                                        San Juan Pueblo.
    The Evergreen Rain God is moving.
The Yellow-leaf Rain Maiden is moving.

Slow Standing Dance
Here toward summer, Yellow Bird Youths are
                                    singing beautifully.
    Here toward summer, Yellow Bird Maidens sing softly.
Butterfly Youths are perched on top of the blossoms.
    Butterfly Maidens are hovering over the blossoms.
Rain God Youths are singing.
    Rain God Maidens are humming.

Fast Kneeling Dance
Rain God Youths are singing.
    Rain God Maidens are humming.
San Juan youths are shaking their rattles, shaking them.
    San Juan maidens are swaying their dew baskets,
                                        swaying them.
The Rain Gods are coming, they're coming.

At a place in the north, cloud flowers.
At a place in the west, cloud flowers.

The San Juan youths are shaking their rattles.
 The San Juan maidens are swaying their dew baskets.
The Rain Gods are coming.

At a place in the south, cloud flowers.
At a place in the east, cloud flowers.

Slow Standing Dance
 In our fields, corn flowers are there.
Above the plants, Hummingbird Boys are hovering.
 In our fields, corn flowers are there.
Above the plants Hummingbird Girls are making their sounds.

 Here, butterflies, there are blue butterflies
above the flowers, yellow butterflies above the flowers.
 Beautifully, they are coming.

 The Rain God Youths are singing.
The Rain God maidens are making their sounds.
 The blue butterflies, the yellow butterflies
are above the flowers.
 Blue butterflies and yellow butterflies,
beautifully, they appear above the flowers.

TEWA ENTRANCE SONG

I: Kosa
From years back, east, on the outskirts
of the pueblo, at Blue Sun Lake,
kosa men are singing beautifully,
beautifully singing.

II: Summer Cacique
Who asked me to gather flowers?
Dark Corn Girls asked me to gather yellow flowers.
Who is urging me on?
Yellow Corn Boys, Yellow Corn Boys,
they are urging me to gather dark flowers.

III: Winter Cacique
Clouds are over the kiva
here at San Juan.
The Cloud Rain God has flowers here.
And then it rains at San Juan.

IV: Bear Society
In the turquoise village
I made this dance kilt
and this white embroidered manta.
I made them quickly.
I have medicinal herbs.

V: Kwirana
Lots of clowns,
lots of watermelons,
lots of muskmelons.
We planted,

we harvested,
we offered.

VI: Game Priest
Somewhere at Deer Lake
Deer Cloud Boys are singing
beautifully.
In the middle,
flowers are blooming
beautifully.

VII: Officers
Star flower baskets.
In the heavens are baskets.
They are eagle tails.
They are parrot tails.

VIII: Women's Society
Speckled Corn Maidens
carry dew baskets
on their heads.
They will receive fertility
because they are female.

X: Summer Moiety
The Shiwana are singing.
Beyond the pueblo at Lake Atsikuma
the summer oxua boys have made things beautiful.
Summer oxua girls have made flowers.

XI: Winter Moiety
Beyond the pueblo at Flower Lake
Flower Rain Gods, boys, girls,
are making beautiful sounds.
With their breath they are producing
white and red flowers.

ONE-EYED FORD

We ya ho

When the dance is over, sweetheart,
I'll take you home
in my one-eyed Ford.

We ya he

SAYATECA'S MORNING CHANT

And now it has come to pass.
This past day I stood beside the water-filled ladder
of my daylight fathers,
of my daylight mothers
and daylight children.
We who were standing
in the rain-filled room
of our daylight fathers
stayed there quietly till dawn.
Now our dawn fathers,
dawn old men,
dawn young men,
dawn boys,
dawn old women,
dawn matrons,
dawn maidens,
dawn girls,
have risen at their sacred place
and have come to meet us now.
There in the rain-filled rooms
of your daylight fathers,
your daylight mothers,
you have stayed all night.
Finally, my children,
make haste, get ready.
Yesterday, whichever of your daylight fathers
wished to grow old worked on plume wands
until evening.
And our mothers,
whoever wished to grow old,
in order to add to the hearts of their ancestors,
and their children,
sat weary by the fireplaces

until evening.
With aching knees,
and sweat running down their faces,
with burned fingers,
they sat weary until evening came.
And whoever else wished to grow old
prepared prayer meal
and gave it to us.
Taking only this
and the plume wands they gave us,
along with the food they cooked for us
and gave us to take along,
taking only this
we shall go out,
with the song cycles of our fathers over there,
life-giving priests,
life-giving pekwins,
life-giving bow priests.
We danced the whole night.
Now hurry, my children,
hurry now,
get ready.
At the new year
all my fathers
with their precious plume wands
appointed me.
There to the south
following the roads of my fathers, came out
rainmakers, priests.
I continue to give my own
poorly made plume wands to my fathers.
And when the cycle of their months was at an end,
meeting my fathers at a spring called
Ayayaka since the first beginning,
I gave them plume wands.
The days having been counted
there in the west,
where my father's road comes in,
I continued to give them plume wands.

When all these days were past
the one who is my father
took hold of me.
Where he had prepared a seat
four times he sprinkled prayer meal on it.
Four times he sprinkled
the top of my head.
When his seat was set
he took hold of me.
Presenting me to all the directions
he made me sit down.
Taking his grandson,
Reed Youth, within his body,
four times he bored a hole through.
Four times drawing toward him his bag of tobacco
he put his hand in.
Into the palm of his hand
four times he measured out tobacco.
He pulled the mist four times
into his body.
He took his grandmother by the hand.
Inhaling four times he drew the mist through.
Into his body he drew the misty breath.
On all sides, all around, with mist
he added to the hearts of his fathers.
He handed it to me.
Inhaling four times I made the mist pass through me.
I drew the mist into my body.
So the rainmakers don't withhold their misty breath
I added mist to their hearts.
When all this was done we greeted each other
with terms of kinship:
father, son; elder brother, younger brother;
uncle, nephew; grandfather, grandson; ancestor, descendant.
We greeted one another with many words.
When it was all over
my father questioned me:
"Now it seems you have something to say,
a word or two, not too long. If you

let me know it I shall know it for all time."
"Yes, that is so. There to the south,
following where my fathers' watery roads come out,
I have been asking for light for you.
Yesterday we reached the appointed time.
Perpetuating the rite of the one who is our father,
Sayateca, bow-priest,
and once more giving him human form,
I came out. Standing upright,
I looked to the north.
I looked to the west,
I looked to the south,
I looked to the east.
Toward the place of dawn
I saw four roads side by side.
Along the middle road
I sprinkled prayer meal four times.
Then I made the sound of
the water-filled breath of the rainmaker priest of the north.
Taking four steps, four times striding forward,
I stood beside the water-filled woodpile
of my daylight father.
Four times my father sprinkled my head
with prayer meal.
He sprinkled his rain-filled woodpile with meal.
After he'd finished I sprinkled my prayer meal on it too.
Tonight the thoughts of all my fathers,
whatever they wished when they appointed me
with their precious plume wand,
I have fulfilled.
The breath of my father,
Sayateca, bow-priest,
his life-giving breath,
his breath of old age,
his breath of waters,
his breath of fecundity,
his breath of seeds,
his breath of riches,
his breath of power,

his breath of strong spirit,
his breath of all manner of good fortune,
I ask for his breath
and draw it into my body.
Now I add to your breath.
In addition, the yellow clothing bundle of the
                                    priest of the north,
the blue clothing bundle of the priest of the west,
the many-colored clothing bundle of the priest of the Above,
the dark-colored clothing bundle of the priest of the Below,
and all kinds of good fortune—
asking for the breath of these
I inhale the breath into my body
and add to your breath.
So, my children, may you be blessed with light.
May your roads be accomplished.
May you grow old.
May your roads reach out there
to where the road of your sun father comes out.
Together may your roads be fulfilled.

THEY WENT TO THE MOON MOTHER

The two stars are saying this
to all the scared bundles here:
"Rejoice! Holy bundles, sacred bundles, because of your
wise thoughts your Moon Mother spoke, gave her word.
Rejoice! You will be granted many blessings, flowing silt."

Maskers, rainmakers
soaking the earth with rain,
making lightning, stretching, stretching.

I, the masker, say this to you:
"By the Moon Mother's word
from the Middle Place all the way to Dawn Lake
your paths will be complete,
you will reach old age."

HOPI BAREFOOT KACHINA DANCE SONG

It has rained on your grandfather's cornfield,
    my dear grandchildren.

Everything has become shiny with water.
    So we'll go channel water to those plants

that need it, and then we'll all go to swim,
    all day, right there!

We'll go to your grandfather's cornfield, and
    when we get there we'll see all the pretty colors.

Walking along through the corn plants, looking around,
    we'll see lots of corn tassels, and ears filling out.

We'll go look at the watermelon plants and the
    muskmelon plants with their little globes

sitting among the runners.
    Yes, we are happy. Yes!

SONG OF THE LOCUSTS

My fathers, my mothers,
with our earth-colored flutes, our blue flutes,
in summer a beautiful life
will begin for us.
In summer blossoms wave,
in summer blossoms sway.

Then the good locusts, the White Earth Locust Youths,
will bring a beautiful life for all in summer.
In summer blossoms wave,
in summer blossoms sway.

HOPI EAGLE DANCE

the eagle rises
earth and heaven are one
his plumes filled with prayer
the great bird moves
up into the sky
its wings sweeping upward
The eagle rises

HOPI BUTTERFLY DANCE SONG

Come here, Thunder, and look!
Come here, Cold, and see it rain!

Thunder strikes and makes it hot.
All seeds grow when it is hot.

    Corn in blossom.
    Beans in blossom.

You face the garden, and look.
    Watermelon plants,
    muskmelon plants.
You face the garden, and look.

SONG *FROM* THE MOUNTAIN CHANT

the voice that makes the land lovely
again and again it sounds
among the dark clouds
the thunder's voice
the voice above
The voice that makes the land lovely

The voice that makes the land lovely
the voice below
the voice of the grasshopper
among the little plants
again and again it sounds
the voice that makes the land lovely

PRAYER OF THE FIRST DANCERS
FROM THE CEREMONY OF THE NIGHT CHANT

O, you who live in Tsegíhi,
in the house made of dawn,
in the house made of evening twilight,
in the house made of dark cloud,
in the house made of male rain,
in the house made of female rain, in the house made of pollen,
in the house made of grasshoppers,
where dark mist drops over the door
to which the path on the rainbow stretches,
where the zigzag lightning stands high,
where the male rain stands high,
O, male god,
with your shoes of dark cloud, come to us,
with your leggings of dark cloud, come to us,
with your shirt of dark cloud, come to us,
with your headdress of dark cloud, come to us,
with your mind enveloped in dark cloud, come to us.
With the dark thunder above you, high-flying, come to us.
With the shaped cloud at your feet, high-flying, come to us.
With the distant darkness made of dark cloud over your head,
                                        come to us.
With the distant darkness made of male rain over your head,
                                        come to us.
With the distant darkness made of female rain over your head,
                                        come to us.
With the zigzag lightning flung out high over your head,
                                        come to us.
With the rainbow hanging high over your head, come to us.
With the distant darkness made of dark cloud on the
                                tips of your wings,
                                        come to us.
With the distant darkness made of the male rain at the

                         tips of your wings, flying high,
                                   come to us.
With the distant darkness made of the dark mist at the
                         tips of your wings, flying high,
                                   come to us.
With the distant darkness made of the female rain at the
                         tips of your wings, flying high,
                                   come to us.
With the zigzag lightning flung out high on the tips
                         of your wings, come to us.
With the rainbow hanging high on the tips of your wings,
                                   come to us.
With the near darkness made of the dark cloud, of
         the male rain, of the dark mist, of the female rain,
                                   come to us.
With the darkness of the earth, come to us.
With these I wish for the foam floating on the water
                    flowing over the roots of the great corn.
I have made sacrifice for you.
I have prepared smoke for you.
Restore my feet for me.
Restore my limbs for me.
Restore my body for me.
Restore my mind for me.
Restore my voice for me.
Take your spell out for me today.
Take your spell away for me today.
You have taken it away from me.
It is taken far away from me.
You have taken it far off.
In beauty I recover,
in beauty my inside becomes cool.
In beauty my eyes regain their sight.
In beauty I regain the use of my limbs.
In beauty I hear again.
In beauty the spell is lifted.
In beauty I walk.
Impervious to pain, I walk.

My insides light, I walk.
I walk with lively feelings.
In beauty, I desire abundant dark clouds.
In beauty, I desire dark mists.
In beauty, I desire passing showers.
In beauty, I desire plants of all kinds.
In beauty, I desire pollen.
In beauty, I desire dew.
In beauty, may lovely white corn accompany you to the ends
of the earth.
In beauty, may lovely yellow corn accompany you to the ends
of the earth.
In beauty, may lovely blue corn accompany you to the ends
of the earth.
In beauty, may corn of all kinds accompany you to the ends
of the earth.
In beauty, may beautiful plants of all kinds accompany you
to the ends of the earth.
In beauty, may beautiful goods accompany you to the ends
of the earth.
In beauty, may beautiful jewels accompany you to the ends
of the earth.
With these in front of you, may they come with you in beauty.
With these in front of you, in beauty may they come with you.
With these behind you, may they come with you in beauty.
With these below you, may they come with you in beauty.
With these above you, may they come with you in beauty.
With these all around you, may they come with you in beauty.
In this way you accomplish your tasks in beauty.
Old men will look at you happily.
Young men will look at you happily.
The young women will look at you happily.
The boys will look at you happily.
The girls will look at you happily.
The children will look at you happily.
The chief men will look at you happily.
Happily, dispersing in different directions, they will
look at you.

Happily, as they approach their homes, they will regard you.
Happily, may their roads home be on the trail of pollen.

Again I walk in beauty,
with beauty before me,
with beauty behind me,
with beauty below me.
With beauty above me,
with beauty all around me, I walk.

It is finished again in beauty.
It is finished again in beauty.
It is finished again in beauty.
It is finished again in beauty.

FIRST SONG OF THE THUNDER

Above
a voice
the voice of the thunder
inside the black cloud
again and again
that wandering voice

Below
a voice
the voice of the grasshopper
in among the plants
again and again
that wandering voice

TWELFTH SONG OF THE THUNDER

Above
the voice of the thunder
inside the black cloud
that voice again
moving about
the voice that fills the land with beauty

Below
the voice of the grasshopper
in among the plants
that voice again
moving about
the voice that fills the land with beauty

It hangs
        a curtain
    Daylight Boy
from the place of daylight
    before him   as night passes away
from behind him
    in a beautiful way
from his voice
    it is hanging

It hangs
        a curtain
    Daylight Girl
from the land of day's yellow light
    before her   as night passes away
from behind her
    in a beautiful way
from her voice
    it is hanging

THE MAKING OF THE GAME ANIMALS

One of the gods is thinking where it will be made. He is
    thinking of it in the center of First Man's House.
In the center of Stretchable House, someone is thinking of it;
    where the finest game animals will be made, someone is
                thinking of this.
    Someone is thinking of this on a floor of soft goods;
on a floor of jewels, he is thinking of this.
    Someone is thinking of where its feet shall be made,
            and how,
under them, the dew, and the pollen of all plants
            shall be made.
    Someone is thinking of where its legs shall be made, how
these shall be made with sunrays.
    Someone is thinking of where its body shall be made,
            how it
shall be made with dark clouds and male rain. Someone
            is thinking
    of where its mind shall be, how it shall be made
of dark wind.
    Someone is thinking where its speech and voice shall be,
how straight lightning shall come into being with its voice.
    Someone is thinking how the front of its body shall be
made beautiful, and how the back of its body shall be
    made beautiful. Someone is thinking how it shall become
the Long Life Being. Someone is thinking where
            it will be made.
    Someone is thinking of it in the center of
            First Woman's House.
Someone is thinking about it in the center of
            Stretchable House
    where the first game animals shall be made.
Someone is thinking about it on a floor of jewels,
    on a floor of soft goods.

Someone is thinking of where its feet shall be made, and how,
    under them, the dew, and the pollen of all plants,
                             shall be made.
Someone is thinking of where its legs shall be made, how they
    shall be made with the sun's reflected red.
Someone is thinking of where its body shall be made, how it
    shall be made of dark mist and female rain.
One is thinking where its mind shall be made, how it will
    be made with blue wind.
One is thinking where its speech and voice shall be made,
    how straight lightning shall come into being with its voice.
One is thinking how the back of its body shall be
                             made beautiful,
    how the front of its body shall be made beautiful.
One is thinking how it shall become the Long Life Being,
    the Happiness Being.
Someone is speaking of it. Now somebody has laid it down.
    Now somebody is giving it shape. Now somebody
                           has finished
making it. Now it is moving. In the rear of First Man's House
    it is moving. On a floor of soft goods it is moving,
on a floor of jewels. Now it is moving its foot, carefully.
    It is moving among dew and pollen of all kinds of plants.
Its legs are now moving, it is moving with sunrays.
    Its body is moving, with dark clouds and male rain
                        it is moving.
Its mind now is moving, with dark wind it is moving.
    Its speech and voice are moving; with the voice of straight
lightning it is moving.
    The front of its body is beautiful now it is moving;
                        the back
of its body is beautiful now it is moving.
    Now Long Life Being, now Happiness Being is
                         indeed moving.
In the back of First Woman's House it is moving, in the back
    of Stretchable House it is moving.
On a floor of jewels, it is moving. On a floor of soft goods,
    it is moving.
Its foot is moving carefully; among the dew on plants

and pollen of all kinds it is moving.
It is moving with the sun's reflected red, with dark mist
    and female rain it is moving.
Now its mind is moving, it moves with blue wind,
    its speech and voice move.
The back of its body is beautiful as it moves,
    the front of its body is beautiful as it moves.
Now Long Life Being, now Happiness Being is indeed moving.
    Now it has stood up. Now it has started to walk. The back
of its body is beautiful as it starts to walk,
    the front is beautiful now it has started to walk.
All its surroundings are beautiful as it starts to walk,
    its words are beautiful now it has started to walk.
Now it is Long Life Being, Happiness Being,
    now it has started to walk.

CHIEF HOGAN SONGS

No. 1
I know how it is, how it goes. . . .
Now my hogan's stones are set under the doorposts
it has come into being. I know.
"Is that right?" they ask. I'm the one who knows.
Now my doorway, now my woven curtain
has come into existence. I know.
"Is that right?" they ask. I'm the one who knows.
Now long life and happiness have come into being.
I'm the one who knows.
My fire, my food, have come into being.
Now long life and happiness have come into being.
My fire, my food, have come into being.
The stirring stick, the large pot have come into being.
The big horn ladle, the big earthen bowl have come into being.
The whiskbroom, the millstone have come into being.
My bed, my woven matting have come into being.
In my hogan, in the back corners, all kinds
of precious fabrics, all kinds of jewels were brought in.
"Is that right?" they ask. I'm the one who knows.
Now long life and happiness have come into being.

No. 14
From a woman, from a woman,
it is my hogan where from the rear corners beauty radiates;
from the rear corners beauty radiates; it radiates
from a woman.
It is my hogan where from the rear center beauty radiates;
it radiates from a woman.
It is my hogan where from the fireside beauty radiates;
it radiates from a woman.
It is my hogan where from its side corners beauty radiates;
it radiates from a woman.

It is my hogan where, from the doorway, going on and on,

beauty

radiates, it radiates from a woman, its span of beauty spreads.

HOW CHANGING WOMAN WAS PICKED UP

On the summit of Gobernador Knob he found her,
Talking God found her, Changing Woman.
Dark cloud, male rain, rainbow, and collected waters
were there where he found her.
The Corn Beetle's frequent call with its pretty voice was there
when he found her. As Long-life Happiness he found her.
Before her it was blessed, behind her it was blessed,
when he found her, when he found her.

On the summit of Gobernador Knob he found her.

Calling God found her, he found Changing Woman.
Dark mist, female rain, sunray, and water's child were there
when he found her.
The small dark bird's frequent call with its pretty voice
was there when he found her.
Behind her it was blessed, before her it was blessed
when he found her, when he found her.
As Long-life Happiness he found her.

DAWN SONG

There is a thrill in its call, it calls to me,
    Crystal Boy; it calls to me.
To the summit of Blanca Peak it calls to me.
    Now it is Talking God Boy who calls to me.
A small bluebird is his head plume,
    at its tip a corn beetle sways as he calls to me,
its call frequent, its voice beautiful, calling to me.

I step in pollen as it calls to me.
A rainbow of dark colors encircles me, as it calls,
    and various fabrics fall over me, as it calls.
It encircles me with pollen, keeping it invisible,
    as it calls to me. Before me is blessed, behind me
                                                  is blessed,
as it calls to me, a thrill in its call to me.
    It calls to me, Boy-who-returns-with-single-turquoise.
There is a thrill in its call to me.
    To the summit of Mount Taylor it calls to me.
Now it is Calling God Boy who calls to me.
    His head plume is a corn beetle. At its tip
a small bluebird sways as he calls to me.
    Its call is frequent, its voice beautiful, as it calls to me.
I walk in corn beetles as it calls to me.
    A blue rainbow encircles me as it calls,
and the jewels with it encircle me as it calls to me.
    With pollen keeping it invisible, it encircles me
as it calls to me.
    Now I am long life, happiness, as it calls to me.
Behind me is blessed as it calls to me.
    Before me is blessed as it calls to me.
There is a thrill in its call to me.

SONG OF THE EARTH

The Earth is beautiful.
The Earth is beautiful.
The Earth is beautiful.

Below the East, the Earth, its face toward the East.
The top of its head is beautiful.
The soles of its feet are beautiful.
Its feet, they are beautiful.
Its legs, they are beautiful.
Its body, it is beautiful.
Its chest, its breast, its head feather,
they are beautiful.

Below the West, the Sky, its face toward the West.
The top of its head is beautiful.
The soles of its feet are beautiful.
Its feet, they are beautiful.
Its legs, they are beautiful.
Its body, it is beautiful.
Its chest, its breast, its head feather,
they are beautiful.

Below the East, the Dawn, its face toward the East.
The top of its head is beautiful.
The soles of its feet are beautiful.
Its feet, they are beautiful.
Its legs, they are beautiful.
Its body, it is beautiful.
Its chest, its breast, its head feather,
they are beautiful.

Below the West, the afterglow of sundown, its face
toward the West,

is beautiful.
Below the East, White Corn, its face toward the East,
    is beautiful.
Below the South, Blue Corn, its face toward the South,
    is beautiful.
Below the West, Yellow Corn, its face toward the West,
    is beautiful.
Below the North, Varicolored Corn, its face toward the North,
    is beautiful.
Below the East, Sahanahray, its face toward the East,
    is beautiful.
Below the West, Bekayhozhon, its face toward the West,
    is beautiful.
Below the East, Corn Pollen, its face toward the East,
    is beautiful.
Below the West, the Corn Beetle, its face toward the West,
    is beautiful.

The Earth is beautiful.
The Earth is beautiful.
The Earth is beautiful.

FATHER BERARD HAILE, *Prayer Stick Cutting in a Five-Night Navajo Ceremonial*

BATHING SONG

Dark thunder is spreading with dark cloud,
his feet are keystone clouds, gathered water his means of travel,
                                              dark mist his body,
sun bars lie on his body, his face is pollen, his voice
                                              corn beetle's,
from his wingtips twelve zigzag lightning bolts flash
                                              back and forth,
from his wingtips twelve dark water jugs hang in a row,
from his wingtips small blue birds usually chirp,
from his wingtips water sprays up; in beauty
he restores your mind, he restores your voice, he restores
                                              your head.

DAWN SONG

Dawn
I am,
white Coyote
I am,
a white tail feather is attached to me,
it's my offering that's attached to me,
at white horizontal streak
I travel.

Evening twilight
I am,
yellow Coyote
I am,
a yellow tail feather is attached to me,

it's my offering that's attached to me,
at yellow horizontal streak
I travel.

Horizontal blue
I am,
blue Coyote
I am,
a blue tail feather is attached to me,
it's my offering that's attached to me,
at horizontal blue streak
I travel.

Darkness
I am,
dark Coyote
I am,
a dark tail feather is attached to me,
it's my offering that's attached to me,
at horizontal black streak
I travel.

Now at dawn when changing Coyote
had tossed his eyes up into a pine tree,
he ran under it. Squatting there,
he kept saying, Drop back into my eye sockets!

Now, at the passing of the night,
Chickadee kept tossing his eyes
into a needle spruce. He'd
run below it, squat, and say,
Drop back into my eye sockets!

THE PRAYER OF SLIM WOMAN

Head Mountain! Head Mountain!
Black Wind! Splendid Leader!
Let a rainbow run from the tips of your fingers,
thrust out a rainbow from your brow,
a rainbow from the palm of your hand
for me to walk on.
Black wind and black clouds,
blue wind and blue clouds,
yellow wind and yellow clouds,
white wind and white clouds—
all of you run ahead of me and darken the sun.
Let me walk wrapped in your cloud garments.
Let it rain peacefully before me;
let the corn ripen,
the white corn, the yellow, the blue.
Earth woman, send rain,
the rain, kind and gentle,
so all may be happiness before me,
so all may be harmony behind me,
so all may be beauty all around me. . . .

Now all is harmony, all is happiness.

KINAALDÁ RACING SONGS

I
Her child,
the sounds have faded in the distance,
the sounds have faded into the distance.

Child of the West,
the sounds have faded into the distance.
Turquoise Girl,
the sounds have faded into the distance.
Her turquoise shoes,
the sounds have faded into the distance.
Surrounded by Earth People,
the sounds have faded into the distance.
Mountains of jewels encircle her,
the sounds have faded into the distance.
All kinds of vegetation follow her in one direction as she runs,
the sounds have faded into the distance.
Now the sound of small yellow speckled birds is heard
above her,
the sounds have faded into the distance.
Behind her night has now passed away,
the sounds have faded into the distance.
Before her night has now passed away,
the sounds have faded into the distance.
Behind her, it is blessed,
the sounds have faded into the distance.
Before her, it is blessed,
the sounds have faded into the distance.
Now the girl can endure much without tiring,
the sounds have faded into the distance.

II

The breeze coming from her as she runs,
   the breeze coming from her as she runs,
     the breeze coming from her as she runs
     is beautiful.

Black Jewel Girl,
   the breeze coming from her as she runs is beautiful.
Her black jewel shoes,
   the breeze coming from her as she runs is beautiful.
Her dark-seamed, black-jewel shoes,
   the breeze coming from her as she runs is beautiful.
Her black-jewel shoestrings,
   the breeze coming from her as she runs is beautiful.
Her black-jewel leggings,
   the breeze coming from her as she runs is beautiful.
Her black-jewel garters,
   the breeze coming from her as she runs is beautiful.
Her black-jewel skirt,
   the breeze coming from her is beautiful.
Her black-jewel skirt sash,
   the breeze coming from her is beautiful.
Her black-jewel clothes,
   the breeze coming from her is beautiful.
Her black-jewel armband,
   the breeze coming from her is beautiful.
Her black-jewel bracelet,
   the breeze coming from her is beautiful.
Her black-jewel collar,
   the breeze coming from her is beautiful.
A black-jewel rock crystal, now she has put it on,
   the breeze coming from her is beautiful.
Her black-jewel ear pendant, now she has put it
                   on her forehead.
   the breeze coming from her is beautiful.
A perfect black jewel, now she has put it on her forehead,
   the breeze coming from her is beautiful.
Her black-jewel head plume, now she has put it on,
   the breeze coming from her is beautiful.

All kinds of horses come up to her and flow by,
    all kinds of sheep,
all kinds of wild game,
    all kinds of vegetation,
the breeze coming from her is beautiful.

    Beautiful people to serve her,
all kinds of jewels,
    all kinds of soft fabrics,
the breeze coming from her is beautiful.

In long life, in everlasting beauty,
    the breeze coming from her is beautiful.
Beauty being with her, it stretches as far as the horizon,
    increasing without blemish,
the breeze coming from her is beautiful.

Before, behind, it is blessed,
    the breeze coming from her is beautiful.

The breeze coming from her as she runs,
the breeze coming from her as she runs,
the breeze coming from her as she runs
is beautiful.

HOPI VIRGINS SEDUCED

I have changed into Marsh-plant Youth.
 The sun's red plume is my head plume, the light
         surrounding the sun
surrounds me now.
 The marsh plant, whose petal tips are dark, whose flowers
are white, whose flowers are blue, whose flowers
 are yellow, whose flowers are variegated,
I hold it up to the Hopi girl.
 In the rear corner of her house, she began to think.
Then she rose.
 Her thought went to the center of her home. Following it,
she walked there, and stood still.
 Her thought went to the fireside of her home. She
           followed it
there, and stood still.
 Her thought went to the side corner of her home.
         She followed it
there, and stood still.
 Her thought went to the path leading from her house.
She walked toward it.
 Black spots appeared before her eyes, then white spots,
then blue, then yellow. In front of her eyes various colors
 appeared. And when she gazed out she felt a thrill
run through her, again and again. At her ankle a rainbow
 will appear. It did appear, on her. Along the path
leading from her house, the rainbow continues to move
 along with her. Away from the house, but still
in sight of it, on top of a ridge, it has moved up with her.
 Along the path leading straight toward my house,
it continued to move along with her.
 Along the path leading toward my door, it continued
to move along with her.

Along the corners of my home, it began to move
along with her.
Along the fireside of my home, it continued to move with her
to the center of my home. It continued to move with her
to the rear corner of my home, it continued to move with her.
When she gazed upon my head plume, a thrill
went through her.
The pollen of my head plume made her dizzy.
Her feet became like my feet, my legs became
like her legs, her body became similar to my body.
My mind and her mind became similar, her speech
and my speech,
my voice and her voice, her laughter and my laughter
became similar, my eyes and her eyes, her skull
and my skull,
her head and my head became similar, my hair and her hair
became alike, her means of travel and mine became alike.

SONGS OF THE MOUNTAIN SPIRIT CEREMONY

VI

The Great Blue Mountain Spirit in the east,
his body, his spirit's vigor, is made of the
blue mirage in the center of the sky.
My songs about it have been made.
He is happy with me.
My songs have been made on the earth.
The Great Yellow Mountain Spirit in the south,
his home is made of yellow clouds,
his body, his spirit's vigor, is made of them.
By means of them he sings into my mouth,
and then the ceremony on the earth has begun.
The Great White Mountain Spirit in the west,
his home is the cross of white clouds in the center
of the sky.
He is happy with me. There is a ceremony,
and my songs about it have been made.
The Great Black Mountain Spirit in the north,
he is happy with me.
My songs have been made.
He sings the ceremony into my mouth.
I am happy with it.
My songs about it have been made.

VII

The Great Blue Mountain Spirit in the east,
the Holy Mountain Spirit, the leader of the Mountain Spirits,
the home above the sky,
the cross of turquoise,
there the ceremony has begun.
I am happy with it. He is happy with it.
The tips of his horns are made of the yellow foot dust

of the Mountain Spirits.

Because of them, one can see in all directions.

In the south, the topmost house is made of yellow clouds,
that's where the Great Yellow Mountain Spirit lives.

The yellow clouds are moving downward toward me,
and the turquoise cross.

The ceremony has begun.

The house of the Great White Mountain Spirit in the west
is made of white clouds,
and the cross made of turquoise.

The ceremony has begun.

I am happy with it. He is happy with it.

The people have been created.

The Great Black Mountain Spirit in the north
is made of black clouds, his body
is made of the black mirage,
the turquoise cross.

The ceremony has begun.

He is happy with me. I am happy.

SONG FOR A BABY CARRIER

A good long life plays over it, back and forth.
It is made of white water below, in a circle, they say.
They say it is made of white water that spreads across it.
They say it's made of white shell that curves over the head.
They say lightning dances alongside,
lightning that fastens across, they say.
They say it's carried by ropes of the rainbow.
A blanket of black water covers all,
and a white water blanket.
It is made of long good life, they say.
They say the sun rumbles inside.

SONG OF THE EASYGOING WOMEN

The heart of the easygoing woman
    has gone out of her
        and is running about in the distance
           running through the long hours of darkness

        giving her light

Those playful women!
Those playful women!
    How did they get so dizzy?
They've made my own heart drunk,
    those little playful women!
        Since they're so dizzy
           perhaps they'll take me with them.

        Yes, wild women
           are seizing my heart
              and leading me off to the west—
           I like it!
        One each side,
        they are taking me somewhere.

              [sung by the women]

        A dizzy man has grabbed me
        and is taking me over there.
        Darkness falls in my way.
        I don't know what to do.

SPEECH BEFORE BUTCHERING THE DEER

My desire fulfilled itself
in thick straw.
With it I made an image, finished it.
It was the rainbow.
With it I made hind legs.
It was the Milky Way.
With it I made the forelegs.
It was the wind.
With it I stroked the image
and water dripped from it.

It was thick straw.
I placed it in my head as horns.
I made the ears of broad leaves,
then folded up the wind
to make a snout.
It was hail,
and I made eyes.
It was a cloud
I pressed onto the buttocks as a tail.
Then I made hair.
It was the wind.
With it I stroked the image
and water dripped from it,
and I let the deer go.

A mountain stood, black, stony.
The deer leaped toward it
and stood behind the gray hill.
Behind the deer was a tree in blossom
which the young men hid behind.
They shot the deer.
Then old men, young men, children,
rubbed themselves with the tail
and prayed for a good life.

QUAIL SONG

Quail children are chattering
     under the bushes.
Coyote quickly tip-
      toes up.
Standing still, he
         flicks his ears
    in all
            directions.

HAVASUPAI MEDICINE SONG

The land we were given
is right here,
right here.
Red rock
streaked with brown
shooting up high
all round our home.
Red rock
shooting up high
right here.
A spring will always be there
down at its foot.
From way back
it is ours.
Right down
the center of our land
a line moves,
bright blue-green.
This is what I'm thinking.
At the edge of the water
cattails appear
bright blue-green,
all round the water.
This is what I'm thinking.
At the edge of the water
foam is forming,
swirling, swirling.
At the edge of the water
silt is being laid down
in ripples.
This is what I'm thinking.
Water skaters walk,

gliding, gliding.
This is what I'm thinking.
Water grasses growing,
bright blue-green
under the water,
waving, waving.
This is what I'm thinking:
Under the water
tiny pebbles.
Flowing over them
the water we drink.
The water is gliding toward the north,
into the distance, beyond our sight.
That is what I'm thinking.
We have arrived here.
An illness.
I sit down,
I sing myself a song.
This is what I'm thinking:
A medicine spirit,
a healer,
I am the same.
An illness.
I sit down.
I sing myself a song.
The things I have named
I leave behind.
This is what I'm thinking.
We arrive there.
We are leaving the canyon.
Out on the rim
horses that are mine,
They roam there
at the junipers,
where the junipers are straight,
and low.
They are right there,
horses that are mine
are gathered there.

This is what I'm thinking.
Here we arrive, then
we swing back down,
moving back down the rocks,
white rocks streaked with brown.
Down at the foot
a spring will always be there,
a spring that heals,
it is right there.
My horses drink the water
that is there.
White rock streaked with brown
shooting up high
is right there.
There is my horse's trail,
zigzagging right down the center,
the color of dust.
It leads to
the source.
It is right here.
That is what I'm thinking.
And now we arrive
down in the canyon,
red rocks,
down in the canyon,
they are right here,
down in the canyon,
red rocks, low down,
they are right here.
Here I walk,
I go alone.
This is what I'm thinking.
Red rocks, streaked with brown,
shooting up high.
It is right here,
down at the foot,
red rocks, boulders
streaked with brown.
They are right here.

My illness is absorbed,
right here.
I will this to be.
I will this to be.

FROM YAQUI DEER DANCE SONGS

I

Little fawn, over there surrounded by flowers
    where the sun rises
        playing in the flower water
          on the flower patio

            Flower fawn
         you are coming to play
      in this flower water

II

I am only a desert melon
in bloom   sending out vines in all directions

    Where are you blooming
                desert melon?

I am sending out vines in all directions

         Over there, where the deer lives
       below the dawn
      it rises in the sky
    a blue cloud   grayish with water

   When it reaches the top
  a soft rain will fall like sparkling mist
on the flower ground

    Where are you blooming
                desert melon?

I am sending out vines in all directions

III

It is time for us sleepy ones to wake up

Let's all wake up   younger brother

       There
               under the dawn
                 on the flower patio
let's all wake up   sleepy ones

IV

When night is fresh you fly up from a mesquite branch
                     over there at the home of the animals
          you fly up   nighthawk
       when night is fresh

V

          Over there
      below the dawn
       among desert scrub
             you lie
        a rasping noise coming from you
                    rotten stick

VI

Who is making the noise of a branch
     breaking on a tree?

            Over there
       below the dawn
     in the scrubby desert
       the whipsnake says
         you do not have a long gray body like mine

VII

What tree is bent over
    with its many blossoms?
        The flower stick is laden with blossoms

                    Over there
              below the dawn
              among the sagebrush
              the *woto boli* can be seen clearly
                                   bending down
                         with the weight of its flowers

VIII
You run ahead of the dust storm
                         enchanted deer
                              making a sacred sound

IX
                 So here you are
                    little brother
           little brother   flower deer
                 Shake your antlers

                 Flower deer
                   why don't you
                 rattle your hoof belt
                   why don't you
                 rustle your
                              cocoon anklets?
           Little brother   flower deer
              shake your antlers
                 little brother

X
                 There seem to be doves
                              over there on the mountain
                 side by side   three gray heads
           bobbing as they walk toward the flower water

                    Over there
                 under the dawn
                 on the mountain there seem to be
                 three gray heads   side by side
                 going toward the flower water

XI

You make a sound like a large animal
                over there
           under the dawn
        At the head of the canyon
         you sound like a large animal

XII

Flower with the body of a fawn
         you are standing beside the cholla
     bending your head to run your antlers
                   on the ground

              Over there
          under the dawn
         beside the cholla you are
 bending your head to rub your antlers
                   on the ground

XIII

        Now the cloud is about to burst
              over there
          under the dawn

   When the blue cloud gray with water
             reaches the top of the sky
      it will let fall a sparkling mist
        that will drop on us
   the cloud is going to burst with a loud noise

//

NOTES

FRANZ BOAS, "Eskimo Tales and Songs," *Journal of American Folklore*, 7, no. 24 (January–March 1894).

"**Shaman's Song**" is my title for Boas' "Song Sung at Religious Festivals in the Singing House" (this and "Song of the Stone" are from Cumberland Sound). The Singing House is the place where festivals are held. Each has a supernatural "owner" with bandy legs, no hair, and no bones in his head. All the words in this song belong to the sacred language of shamans, *angakut*. The song is sung as a chorus to the people assembled. Boas says it is "only an enumeration of animals," but it seems to be a summation of the people's world, with animals at the center. "**Song of the Stone**" is about a stone washed down from the hills by melting waters in spring that becomes the "supernatural helper" of the man who finds it.

KNUD J. RASMUSSEN, *Intellectual Culture of the Copper Eskimos*, trans. W. E. Calvert, *Report of the Fifth Thule Expedition, 1921–24*, vol. 9 (Copenhagen, 1932).

The Copper Eskimo, or Kitlineermuit, are from Victoria Island (Kitlineq). Rasmussen visited a branch called the Umingmaktormuit, the Musk Ox people, and was impressed with "the wonderful poetry." "Never in any other single group," he says, "neither in Greenland, Canada, nor Alaska, have I met such a poetically gifted people." The songs here—"**Old Song of the Musk Ox People**" and "**Song of the Sea**"—were sung by a man named Netsit.

Song is very important in Inuit culture. According to Edmund Carpenter, "The word to make poetry is the word to breathe; both are derivations of *anerca*, the soul, that which is eternal, the breath of life. A poem is words infused with breath or spirit" (quoted in Robin McGrath, "Poetry in the Oral Tradition," chapter 4 of *Canadian Inuit Literature: The Development of a Tradition*, Canadian Ethnology

Service, National Museum of Man Mercury Series, Paper no. 94 [Ottawa, 1984], 43). Rasmussen records in vol. 8, nos. 1–2, that a Netsilik man named Orpingalik said, "All my being is song, and I sing as I draw breath." Clearly, however, on the evidence of some of the poems, some people found it easier to compose than others.

KNUD J. RASMUSSEN, *Intellectual Culture of the Iglulik Eskimos*, trans. W. E. Calvert, *Report of the Fifth Thule Expedition, 1921–24*, vol. 7, no. 1 (Copenhagen, 1929).

"**Avuvnuk's Song**" is from Repulse Bay, Northwest Territories. Avuvnuk was hit by a ball of fire as she went outside to urinate. It entered her body before she could pull up her breeches. She grew light within and lost consciousness. At that moment, she became a great shaman; the spirit of the meteor had entered her. She rushed back into the house singing this song, the song she used thereafter when calling on helping spirits. When the light entered her body she could see, hear, and know everything. At her ceremony, all people confessed their misdeeds and obtained release from them, lifting their arms and flinging the evil away.

In this volume, Rasmussen records a conversation he had with one Ivaluardjuk, who expressed astonishment that in Rasmussen's country there were people who devoted themselves exclusively to the production of poems and melodies. He would not admit that there was any "special art" associated with songs, "but at the most may grant it is a gift, and even then a gift which everyone should possess in some degree" (p. 233). Every person is a singer/poet, as everyone was a craftsperson and so to some extent an artist. One worked on language as one worked on skins or ivory to produce the necessities of life. (For more on Inuit song collected by Rasmussen, see Tom Lowenstein, *Eskimo Poems from Canada and Greenland* [University of Pittsburgh Press, 1973].)

KNUD J. RASMUSSEN, *Observations on the Intellectual Culture of the Caribou Eskimos*, trans. W. E. Calvert, *Report of the Fifth Thule Expedition, 1921–24*, vol. 7, no. 2 (Copenhagen, 1930).

The Caribou Eskimos lived in the interior, on Barren Grounds, and spoke the same language as the Igluliks. "**Song of the Musk Ox**" was sung by Igjugarjuk. It is a freer version of a song he had sung for Rasmussen that omitted certain cultural details obvious to his usual listeners.

Songs of derision were used to expose the faults of villagers. Two men engaged in a public duel of abuse, a kind of "ranking," which sometimes led to fights. In these **Two Songs**, Kakaihuaq derides Utahania.

KNUD J. RASMUSSEN, *Snehyttens Sange* (Gyldendal, Copenhagen, 1961).

These songs were originally published in 1930. *Snehyttens Sange* means "songs from the snow hut," and Rasmussen put the book together from songs he'd published in the *Report of the Fifth Thule Expedition* (1927–30) and *Myter og Sagn fra Groenland*, "Myths and Legends from Greenland" (1921). Tom Lowenstein was the first to translate the latter into English (see note above). I would like to thank Ulla Volk for helping me with the Danish translations.

"The Widow's Song" was sung by the Musk Ox (Copper Eskimo) woman Qernertoq. **"Delight in Nature"** was sung by Tatilgak, also of the Musk Ox people. Both songs were in the *Report of the Fifth Thule Expedition*, but I had overlooked them.

"Song to a Miser" was sung by Angmagssalik from East Greenland. It has a headnote: "Once it was discovered that a man was in the habit of fetching meat from his storage place at night while the others slept. He ate his fill in secret without sharing his enjoyment with those he lived with. As soon as he'd eaten, he wrapped the leftovers in a skin and hid them under the sleeping bench. One of his housemates revenged himself by making the following song, which he recited one evening to the vengeful delight of the audience. It is said that the miser became so ashamed that he never again ate a meal in secret."

"Song to the Spring" was sung by the same person. Rasmussen wrote of this song: "The winter has been long and hard. All the people at the village are exhausted, and there are many who don't believe they'll live to see the spring. Then a man goes out in his kayak along the coast where the first open water has started to form. He comes to a rocky hill, which he climbs to see if there are any openings in the ice further out where he can catch seals. Weak and exhausted from hunger, he climbs the hill until he discovers a snowdrift which the sun's warmth has started to loosen. Then he is so overjoyed he bursts into song."

"Ptarmigan" was sung by Umanatsiaq from West Greenland, and so was **"Lovemaking."**

"**Women's Song Duel**" was from Southern Upernivik, West Green-land. The combatants were Paninguaq (Little Daughter) and her cousin Sapangajagdleq (Pearl).

KNUD J. RASMUSSEN, *The Netsilik Eskimos*, trans. W. E. Calvert, *Report of the Fifth Thule Expedition, 1921–24*, vol. 8, nos. 1–2 (Copenhagen, 1931).

The songs are from Rae Isthmus in the Northwest Territories. The first song was sung by Qaqortingueq, the second by Amatoq, and the third by Piuvkaq. **Amatoq**'s song, as Rasmussen set it down, is not totally comprehensible, maybe because the experience itself is strange and dreamlike and the notes aren't clear. But the singer is on a hunt and standing by a seal's breathing hole, obsessing about women, when some swim by under him and out to sea in the form of seals. He is lonely and doesn't know what to do; he should have given presents to attract them. He symbolizes his awkwardness with his experiences during a caribou hunt "where," in the words of Rasmussen, "amid so many full-grown fat cows, for some reason incomprehensible to him he is content to bring down a little calf" (p. 336). It seems to me, also, that the women become the calf, though there is also something of him in the calf, too. Discussing this song in terms of a vision tradition in *Becoming Half Hidden: Shamanism and Initiation Among the Inuit* (Almqvist and Wiksell International, Stockholm, 1985, pp. 54–57), Daniel Merkur points out that women, seen earlier in the song in the forms of seals, toward the end are seen in the forms of caribou cows.

BEVERLEY CAVANAGH, *Music of the Netsilik Eskimos: A Study in Stability and Change*, Canadian Ethnology Service, National Museum of Man Mercury Series, Paper no. 82, vol. 2 (Ottawa, 1982).

Netsilik is an Inuktitut name meaning "with the seal." The people Cavanagh worked with live around a lake on the Boothia Peninsula in the Northwest Territories.

The performer of "**Siutinuaq's Song**," in 1972, was Martha Kamoo-kak; the composer Siutinuaq was her brother-in-law, and he composed it during hard times. Martha Kamookak summarized the meaning of the song: "The hunter thought he would not succeed in catching any game. When he did get a caribou, he made the song to express his happiness."

"**Luke Uqualla's Song**" was composed about 1920. The song

describes a caribou hunt that started badly, with a thoughtless chase that frightened the animals. The hunter eventually caught up, killed the game, and cached it for future use. Exhausted, he fell asleep. When he woke he continued on his way.

"**Arnaluaq's Song**" was performed by Lucy Avingak Kuptana, but it was composed in the 1920s by her stepfather, Arnaluaq. Note the almost formulaic openings of the songs, referring to their composition. Many Inuit songs are about composing, self-conscious about the process. This song records hunting experiences: a caribou and seal hunt, a ptarmigan chase, and fishing. Cavanagh notes that the ptarmigan and fish seem to be an anticlimactic finish to the hunt, but they might represent caribou and seal, the composer presenting his achievements modestly.

Nicholas Qayutinuaq composed "**Qayutinuaq's Song**" in a dream in the early 1920s, when he was a boy. He could not hunt or play games well, so he had nothing with which to make a song. When an animal appeared, he was successful, but it seems to have disappeared by the final stanza.

Henry Quuksun composed "**Quuksun's Song**" in the 1920s, after his marriage. He was also the singer. It's a challenge song made in response to gossip about him and his wife, who was criticized for not fulfilling her social role satisfactorily. It is interesting, here as elsewhere, to note the connection between successful hunting and successful singing.

"**Iqquqaqtuk's Song**" was sung by Bernard Iqquqaqtuk and composed by him in 1955 when he saw his first plane, a serious agent of change.

RAMON PELINSKI, LUKE SULUK, AND LUCY AMAROOK, *Inuit Songs from Eskimo Point*, Canadian Ethnology Service, National Museum of Man Mercury Series, Paper no. 6 (Ottawa, 1979).

There are no explanations of the **Songs from Eskimo Point** (Northwest Territories), just text, some translations, and music. I conjecture that No. 10 runs together the arrival of a missionary with the missionary's message of the Annunciation. No. 16 seems to be a love song.

THOMAS F. JOHNSON, *Eskimo Music by Region: A Comparative Circumpolar Study*, Canadian Ethnology Service, National Museum of Man Mercury Series, Paper no. 32 (Ottawa, 1976).

These **Inupiat Dance Songs** were collected from Point Hope, northwest Alaska.

Song I refers to whalers camped out on the ice playing checkers, a popular game. The song describes how the loser is required to invent a dance to someone else's song. The final lines turn the tables with humor and ridicule.

Song II is an "inherited dance song" collected in 1973 from Dinah Frankson, who inherited it from her namesake. There is no indication of the song's meaning. I interpret it as hortatory.

In Song III the dance is the whaling feast, *nalukataq*. "Uncle" is a kinship term incorporating distant or non-kin.

Song IV was collected from Dinah and Dave Frankson ("who insisted on being taken to a sound-proof room before agreeing to sing"). We are not provided with enough information to interpret the references to moving rocks and brown and polar bears, but since this is a "juggling-game song" (no description given), and since Johnson gave the song the title "I Move Rocks," one can assume that the references are to the game. There seems to be rivalry indicated between Point Hope and Point Barrow, with its salty water.

MAIJA M. LUTZ, *Musical Traditions of the Labrador Coast Inuit*, Canadian Ethnology Service, National Museum of Man Mercury Series, Paper no. 79 (Ottawa, 1982).

No. I of these **Teasing Songs**, Lutz notes, is a comment on the method of waste disposal in the absence of indoor plumbing.

WALDEMAR JOCHELSON, comp., *Unangam Ungiikangin Kayux Tunusangin / Aleut Tales and Narratives*, ed. Knut Bergsland and Moses L. Dirks, Alaska Native Language Center, University of Alaska (Fairbanks, 1990).

These songs in Appendix A, "Eastern Aleut Song Texts," including "**Love Song I**" and "**Love Song II**," were first published by Ioann Veniaminov in 1846. (In *Coming to Light*, Bergsland has two Aleut translations, a story and a song, from Appendix B in this book, "Atkan Texts." The song is "Song of the Atkan Aleuts.")

The old man of the second song is probably the girl's father. The editors comment on the second love song that "the lovesick singer cannot get enough of his dancing sweetheart's odor."

JEAN MULDER, "Structural Organization in Coast Tsimshian Music," *Ethnomusicology* 38, no. 1 (winter 1994).

Mulder recorded these songs from 1979 to 1981 in Hartley Bay, Kitkatla (Port Simpson), British Columbia.

"**Love Song of Warning**" is from a legend in which a young woman has caught her lover going to meet another woman.

"**Great Blue Heron Children's Song**," sung by Doreen Robinson, is common property. It is chanted, accompanied by body motions imitating a heron in shallow water looking for shellfish. One step is taken with each beat of the music.

"**Little Boy's Mourning Song**" may be from a legend. The boy walks along the beach mourning his dead mother. This song was sung and recorded by a group of women.

"**Billy Goat Song**" is a common song sung by women; there is always much laughter and joking. This song was recorded from a group of elderly women.

FRANZ BOAS, *Kwakiutl Ethnography*, ed. Helen Codere (University of Chicago Press, 1966).

The 1966 volume is made up of Boas' unpublished manuscript, "Kwakiutl Ethnography," along with selections from his other work on the Kwakiutl. Boas' work among this people began in 1885 (he died in 1942), and his work on the potlatch (as indeed most of his Kwakiutl work) was done in close collaboration with the Kwakiutl George Hunt.

The potlatch at this time was a method of acquiring wealth through the distribution of interest-bearing property. Breaking into pieces to give away to rival chiefs, or destroying valuable "coppers" (good-sized ornamental copper plates) was a central part of the ceremonial contest, whose aim was to humiliate a rival or gain prestige over him. The giving of grease feasts was part of this rivalry, which often developed into open enmity. A huge fire was lighted in the center of the house, and etiquette demanded that no one, including the rival chief, move away from the heat. While the feast was in progress, the host sang a song ridiculing his rival. In Song I here, Neqapenkem ("Ten Fathom Face") lets his clan sing first, and then he takes over. Song II is a reply on another occasion by his rival, Henakalaso, who ridicules him for not having returned a grease feast. (In this song, Boas does not explain the insult "spider woman." One supposes the people's faces are dry or moldy because their bellies are empty.)

In Song I Tsonoqoa is a fabulous monster, and the red cedar bark is the emblem of the winter ceremony. The sprinkling of blood refers to the fact that Neqapenkem had killed another chief at a feast, and the thick smoke at the beginning of Song II refers to the fire of the great feast.

The love songs were sung in a way imitating crying, often falsetto and vibrato. Young men's challenging love songs used to be sung by a crowd of young men up and down the village to annoy or embarrass the girls. **"Love Song of a Man Sent to Hunt Goats to Get Tallow for His Beloved"** (tallow was used for cosmetics) may be one of these, and the same with **"Love Song."** Boas notes that many love songs are satirical. In **"Song of a Lover,"** the names the lover calls the woman are the names of the wives of prominent chiefs, so he is claiming high rank for her.

FRANZ BOAS, "Songs of the Kwakiutl Indians," *Internationales Archiv für Ethnographie* 9 (1896).

Boas collected these songs from Vancouver Island. No singers' names are given, and Boas says "the translations do not claim to be perfect."

DIAMOND JENNESS, *The Sekani Indians of British Columbia*, National Museum of Canada Bulletin no. 84, Anthropological Series no. 20 (Ottawa, 1937).

Jenness collected **Caribou Medicine Songs** in the summer of 1924 in northern British Columbia. The Sekani practiced the "vision quest," when a young man at puberty went off for four days and nights, fasting on a mountain, praying. On the fifth day he came down and built a hut near his people, but off by itself. He stayed there from spring until autumn, subject to various restrictions, seeking medicine power through a dream or vision of an animal. With each animal went a song, sung by the animal about itself. Songs or visions were not new, says Jenness. They were inherited "mystically" from some ancestor. Medicine men had a number of these songs, used in healing.

T. F. McILWRAITH, *The Bella Coola Indians*, vol. 2 (University of Toronto Press, 1948).

There had been about twenty villages near the mouth of the

Columbia River in British Columbia. In 1948 there was only one, with some four hundred inhabitants. McIlwraith collected the material from here in 1922 and 1923. He had great difficulty getting accurate versions of songs since "snatches of many are remembered, but few individuals are acquainted with the complete version." He had even more problems with the songs' interpretation. "Songs which have been handed down for generations," he writes, "abound in archaic expressions which are meaningless even to the older men: some recently composed are full of metaphorical devices to conceal their real significance from the uninitiated." However, he continues, "every effort was made to get the *general* meaning." Perhaps some of McIlwraith's difficulties stemmed from his rationalistic and rather condescending attitude—it is clear, for example, that he regards the shamans as little better than quacks and charlatans.

Shaming songs were used primarily to shame runaway wives or husbands. The woman to whom **"Shaming Song for Bushy-Snatch"** is addressed had run away from her husband and got the nickname "Noqwna" ("the one with the very hairy pudenda") conferred at the shaming rite. The second part of the song condemns all the female sex. The third part of the song had been forgotten. The singer was Jim Pollard.

The **"Shaman Song"** was used by Sikwalxwlelix, a woman shaman, and was recorded by Jim Pollard, Reuben Schooner, Talio Charlie, and Steamboat Annie. The word for "salmon" is a word in the language of the supernaturals, the "they." The shaman received some of her power from salmon. The "bowl" is, in the original version, "wash basin" and refers to a "supernatural vessel"; both the water in the vessel and the vessel itself have potency, through association with the supernaturals. It seems that the shaman was carried away by Tlitcaplilana and treated by immersion in a basin in which eagle down had been deposited. (Tlitcaplilana is a supernatural woman who cures and gives both a name and a song to the sufferer, often making him or her a shaman.) Anunitsektnim is a supernatural who restores to life those killed by the receipt of too much power from Tlitcaplilana, as happened to this shaman. At the end, she must have been taken to one of the spots where cures were effected by petrified gods.

"Man's Love Song I," an ancient Bella Coola love song, was sung by Jim Pollard. The Bella Coola envision the sky as a flat surface, similar to earth. Jim Pollard also sang **"Man's Love Song II,"** which he had composed about 1900. The bullhead is an important fish to the Bella Coola and figures in story and myth.

ELIZABETH DERR JACOBS, comp., *Nehalem Tillamook Tales*, ed. Melville Jacobs (University of Oregon Books, 1959; reissued by Oregon State University Press, 1990).

These songs were collected in western Oregon in 1934 from Mrs. Clara Pearson of Garibaldi, a woman in her sixties, one of the few Tillamook survivors to speak the language.

Wild Woman, an important character in myth, had killed Otter for stealing her fish. His family invited her and her husband, Crane, to a feast, intending to take vengeance with the aid of various beasts. But Wild Woman, wearing the otter-skin headdress, knew their plans and planned to counter them with her spirit power. To taunt them she sang **"Wild Woman's Song."** (Crane was ashamed that she mentioned her clitoris, and Otter's four brothers were furious that she'd committed the gross offense of mentioning the dead.) But Wild Woman carried the day and ordained that henceforth nobody could take vengeance during the Winter Dance. She also took the opportunity to note that "in time to come, much later on, some women will not have a clitoris. Such women will not be much good." It is interesting to wonder if Mrs. Pearson would have told a male anthropologist of the many sexual dimensions of Wild Woman (who seems like the female counterpart of Coyote in a number of respects). Thus, in an episode from a story, a woman is paddling a canoe. Mrs. Pearson informed Elizabeth Derr Jacobs that the canoe was Wild Woman's genitals and the paddling was done by her doughty and ubiquitous clitoris.

"Bear's Song" and **"Beaver's Song"** are from "Ahecks Leads a War Party" and are not what they seem. Ahecks, a very large man and something of a skeptic, tested the men in his party to see how strong their supernatural "power" was. "I want to hear your power songs," he told them. Bear sang his (I have gone along with his claim by enacting it "concretely"). "Oh, shut up!" Ahecks said. "All you can do is hunt up a hollow tree and dig it out. That is all you can feel with your paws." Beaver sang his song. "Oh, shut up!" Ahecks said. "All you do is dig mud and build dams and swim around all night. You eat bark. That is all you accomplish." And so on for the others, except Rabbit and Wolf, who pass the test.

FRANZ BOAS, "Chinook Songs," *Journal of American Folklore* 1, no. 1 (April–June 1888).

Chinook is a trade jargon, a lingua franca, that sprang up in Oregon and Washington and spread to Alaska. It was made up of English, French, Chinook (proper), Nootka, and Sahaptin words. Boas collected these **Chinook Songs** in British Columbia in 1886.

Indians lived part of the year in towns and cities along the coast, working in sawmills and canneries, or as sailors, and so on. From time to time they organized feasts where songs were sung, most of them composed by women.

HENRY ROWE SCHOOLCRAFT, "Nursery and Cradle Songs of the Forest," *The American Indians: Their History, Conditions, and Prospects from Original Notes and Manuscripts* (new and revised edition, 1851).

This "arch little song," as Schoolcraft calls **"Ojibwe Cradle Song,"** is in three voices (all, of course, sung by the mother). The baby speaks first, then the owl, then the mother. Schoolcraft gives a few more lullabies and cradle songs and notes that they "constitute . . . rude as they are, and destitute of metrical attractions, a chapter in the history of the human heart, in the savage phasis, which deserves to be carefully recorded." Schoolcraft, who married Jane Johnson, whose father was an Irish fur trader and whose mother was the daughter of the famous Ojibwe chief Wabojeeg, was the first scholar to collect and analyze his materials extensively, and his career inaugurates American ethnology. But he was not interested in the material for its own sake. He was one of many Americans who believed in the march of progress and civilization and wanted to collect evidence of that march, or climb. He was an active supporter of the government's policy of Indian removal.

RICHARD J. PRESTON, *Cree Narrative: Expressing the Personal Meanings of Events*, Canadian Ethnology Service, National Museum of Man Mercury Series, Paper no. 30 (Ottawa, 1975).

These three songs were sung by George Head and collected by Preston on fieldwork conducted among the Eastern Cree of the James Bay area between 1965 and 1969.

"Caribou Hunting Song" is for the start of the fall hunt. The hunter experiences what Preston terms "deep hope," an active feeling the animal will recognize and respond to by waiting for him (the song following in the book is "I see them, waiting for me"). Food animals like to be taken if they are treated with respect. In **"Trapping Song"** (all three song titles are mine), the animal is watching the hunter setting traps, "play," not work, an activity both hunter and hunted enjoy. **"Song for the Muskrat"** is a metaphorical way of saying that the singer will have a close and enduring relationship with the muskrat.

Chapter 6 of *Cree Narrative* is informative on the Cree attitude to hunting, as is Robert Brightman's study *Grateful Prey: Rock Cree Human–Animal Relationships* (University of California Press, 1993).

JAMES MOONEY, *The Ghost-Dance Religion and the Sioux Outbreak of 1890*, Fourteenth Annual Report of the Bureau of American Ethnology, 1892–93, Smithsonian Institution (Washington, D.C., 1896).

The Ghost Dance religion began with the Nevada Paiute prophet Wovoka in 1887. It swept through the Plains around 1890. There are hundreds of Ghost Dance songs from numbers of tribes. Each dance provided many new songs via the dancers' visions, describing experiences in the vision world. "First in importance," says Mooney, "for number, richness of reference, beauty of sentiment, and rhythm of language, are the songs of the Arapaho." The words of Ghost Dance songs are more often than not "cryptic descriptions of visions, fully understood only by the authors" (Demetri B. Shimkin on the Naraya songs [closely related to Ghost Dance songs] of the Wind River Shoshone, quoted in Judith Vander, "Ghost Dance Songs and Religion of a Wind River Shoshone Woman" [Monograph Series in Ethnomusicology, Department of Music, UCLA, 1986]).

In Song I of these **Arapaho Ghost Dance Songs,** the singer met his friends in the spirit world when they were about to go on a great buffalo hunt as in the old days before the whites, when buffalo were plentiful. Song II was composed by Sitting Bull, "the Arapaho apostle of the dance." The Crow is the messenger from the spirit world. The composer of Song III sang this in quick time "to hasten the trance" of his father's transformation; there is another Arapaho song like this where the father transforms into a moose. Song IV contains a doctrine at the core of the Ghost Dance: the restoration of the old, pre-white world. Song V, along with "Paiute Ghost Dance Song," may be the most famous. It summarizes the whole hope of the movement, "the return of the buffalo and the departed dead, the message being brought to the people by the sacred birds, the Eagle and the Crow" (Mooney). In Song VI the Messiah is addressing his children (the

Ghost Dance incorporated Christian ideas). **"Paiute Ghost Dance Song"** contains the doctrine of the new earth that is approaching. The original is "The whirlwind! The whirlwind! / The snowy earth comes gliding." The Ghost Dance died a bloody death at the massacre of Wounded Knee, 1890, when the army's Hotchkiss guns wiped out over two hundred unarmed dancers, mostly women and children. For more on the Ghost Dance, see Michael Hittman, *Wovoka and the Ghost Dance* (Yerington Paiute Tribe, Yerington, Nevada, 1990).

ROBERT H. LOWIE, "Social Life of the Crow Indians," *American Museum of Natural History Anthropological Papers* 9, part 2 (1912).

The only thing Lowie tells us about this popular Crow **"Wolf Lullaby"** is that an ancestor of the singer overheard a female wolf lulling her offspring to sleep with it. I have omitted the last line because I don't understand how it fits in: "The dog gets full, he smokes."

There were two ways of insulting a Crow: to call him a ghost or an orphan. Other ways of getting to him were to sing songs of derision. The story behind the first song goes like this: The Many Lodges division wanted the Black Lodges to join in a revenge raid on the Sioux, but they refused. The Many Lodges went on their own and defeated a band of Sioux, killing twelve. They then returned to the Black Lodges to mock them. The Many Lodges women, whose period of mourning had been terminated by the victory over the Sioux, derided the Black Lodges' chiefs.

For background to **"Gray Bull's Song,"** one needs to know that before Gray Bull became a famous warrior, one winter a mistress told another that she didn't consider him a real man at all. That spring, Gray Bull went on a successful raid and made up this song on his return.

FRANCES DENSMORE, *Pawnee Music* (Da Capo Press, New York, 1972; originally, Smithsonian Institution, Bureau of American Ethnology, Bulletin no. 93 [1929]).

The songs were recorded among the Skidi and Chaui bands near Pawnee, Oklahoma, in 1919 and 1920. **"The Yellow Star"** was sung by Wicita Blain, who said he composed this song on waking from a trance in the Ghost Dance. He dreamed of a yellow star who came to him and said, "I am the star which you see in the sky at night." The star was in the form of a woman holding an eagle feather painted yellow, which she gave to him, saying, "All the stars in the sky are people." She told him to wear the feather upright in his hair.

"The White Fox" was recorded by Wicita Blain and was said to go back to a time when the Pawnee lived in Nebraska, where there were many white and silver foxes. Tradition stated that a war party found a white fox singing this song, which belonged to a warrior society, the Wolf Society.

"Song of the Deer Society" was sung by Mark Evarts. Densmore, the most prolific of all collectors of Native American music and song, says the use of the song was not explained. The Wichita originated the Deer Society (defunct at the time this song was collected), whose ceremonies were held in the fall when the corn was ripe. The purpose was to find out who would be killed on a war party.

GENE WELTFISH, *The Lost Universe: Pawnee Life and Culture* (Basic Books, New York, 1965).

The songs were collected in Pawnee, Oklahoma, between 1928 and 1936. (The original Pawnee home had been in what is now Nebraska; by 1936 their numbers had been reduced from about 12,000 to about 700.)

I made **"Pawnee Love Song"** from Weltfish's note: "They had a song that stated, 'If even worms are inclined to be in love with one another, how can we expect people not to do so?' The statement was startlingly simple and left the implication to be understood. It said, 'Even worms / each other-they them-love.' "

"Awari" is from *"a"* ("being" or "living") and *"wari"* (to go about actively, such as traveling). "The combination *awari*," says Weltfish, "indicates the principles of life and motion *par excellence*, the vigor of life." The Awari or Ground-breaking Ceremony, which included songs and dances by men and woman, had to be performed before planting, just at the time when the first leaves appeared on the willows along the creeks. It also had to wait for the dark of the moon, which signaled the darkness of germination. It is the only Pawnee ceremony in which women played a major role, since it had been invented by a woman, and each year a woman had a vision in which she was told she was the person to see that the ceremony was performed (Weltfish calls her the "visionary").

The ceremony has three intermissions and lasts all day. The breaks come after the second song, after the fifth, and after the seventh. Each song is repeated in at least ten stanzas, or "steps," identical except that for "huraru" ("land," etc., as here), the substitute words symbolize the realms of the universe in the order of their creation, ending with "kiriki," thunder.

Among the ritual items is a special coiled basket made by a woman and carried by the visionary and her assistants. It symbolized the container ordained by Heaven to carry earth from which the world was created and the germs of life. At the time of Creation, Heaven caused the basket to move of itself through space. In the final song, presumably the visionary and her male escort scatter the soil from this basket.

At the beginning of the ceremony, the women stand with hoes ready to scrape the earth. The visionary moves back and forth, "dishing out" earth. In the second song, "the dancers try to flit about like the sparkling stars," since the Evening Star as it appears sparkling and wavering is the power that animates the earth when it generates in darkness. In the third song, "the earth comes sideways from the basket and is endowed with life," while in the fifth "the act of planting is compared to a kind of shooting with the bow and arrow into the earth." The corn/mother/earth symbolism of the sixth song is emphasized the following night when the women plant corn in an even number of hills, thus emphasizing the analogy with their own breasts.

STEVEN J. CRUM, *Po'i Pentun Tammen Kimmappeh / The Road on Which We Came* (University of Utah Press, 1994).

The Western Shoshone people of the Intermountain West call themselves "Newe," People, and the land "Pia Sokopia," Mother Earth. Of these **Two Newe Songs**, Song I was sung by an anonymous Shoshone elder and Song II, "There, in a Distant Place," was translated and transcribed by Beverly Crum of Duck Valley Reservation, Nevada.

FRANCES DENSMORE, *Northern Ute Music* (Da Capo Press, New York, 1972; originally Smithsonian Institution, Bureau of American Ethnology, Bulletin no. 75 [1922]).

This Bear Dance song, which I retitled **"The Red Wagon's Dust,"** was recorded among the White River, Uinta, and Uncompahgre bands of the Ute in White Rocks, Utah, in 1914. The Bear Dance was held in spring, when the bear comes out of hibernation. It might have been a courting dance; when Densmore collected it, it was a dance of "good feeling." Densmore provides no notes on the meaning of this song, but its minimalist feel must have appealed to the imagist poets of the time (Densmore had adapted some of the songs she collected into imagist form, and published them).

EDWARD SAPIR, "Song Recitative in Paiute Mythology," *Journal of American Folklore* 23 (1910).

The songs were collected among the southern Paiutes of southwest Utah and northwest Arizona.

Myth song is very common in Native America. Songs are inserted into the body of the myth to express a character's emotions or a striking thought. The songs are sung or recited.

In this myth, the Mountain Blue Jays ("Blue-Hat People") are helpers of the Badger people in their war with Wolf and Panther. Wolf and Panther retreat to a mountain, while two Mountain Blue Jays "press on and exult."

JOHN FREDERICK KILPATRICK AND ANNA GRITTS KILPATRICK, "Muscogean Charm Songs Among the Oklahoma Cherokee," *Smithsonian Contributions to Anthropology* 2, no. 3 (1967).

There is a tradition that during removal (the Trail of Tears) some Muscogeans joined up with the Cherokee. This **"Muscogean Charm Song"** and others were obtained in 1963 from a Cherokee shaman who had them in a notebook. He assigned them to a Muscogean lineage. The texts are difficult, and the Kilpatricks enlisted the help of a Creek informant in their interpretation and translation. (This text, in fact, may have originally been Cherokee, borrowed from Creeks or Natchez long ago, then returned corrupted to the Cherokee who had long forgotten it.) The Kilpatricks' text is hypothetical, and my version contains conjecture. As I read it, taking my lead from the Kilpatricks, the song is a "hunting charm" meant to "catch" a woman (the fish). She will give herself up. In the second stanza, a rival is disposed of, via charm, and the last line reiterates the theme of the song. (Maybe the fallen rival is now a fish in the stream.)

An important source of Cherokee material is James Mooney, *Sacred Formulas of the Cherokee*, Seventh Annual Report of the Bureau of American Ethnology, 1885–86, Smithsonian Institution (Washington, D.C., 1891).

JAMES MOONEY, *The Swimmer Manuscript: Cherokee Sacred Formulas and Medicinal Prescriptions*, revised, completed, and edited by Frans

M. Olbrechts, Smithsonian Institution, Bureau of American Ethnology, Bulletin 99 (1932).

Swimmer, the compiler of the now-lost manuscript, was Mooney's main informant. He died in 1899. Mooney started work on the manuscript in 1888. This formula was addressed to the stream or river ("Long Person") for the purpose of obtaining long life. The client or medicine man performed the ceremony, the favorite time being at the new moon. The suppliant, often accompanied by his household, goes to the river before sunrise, while still fasting. They cup out water with the hollow of the hand ("I will stretch out my hand"). They wash their hair and breast (where the soul is). The Long Person originated at the cataract, so the reciter claims the same origin, and establishes an intimate relation between himself and the spirit invoked, almost forcing him to pay heed. At the end, the suppliant, having bathed, emerges with white foam on his head, like gray hair. Taking the white walking stick (an attribute of old people or chiefs), he starts on his journey to the seventh upper world (that is, the summit of human happiness). He will live to be old, beside the burning hearth. (For further information on this ceremony, see Mooney's "The Cherokee River Cult," *Journal of American Folklore*, volume 12 [January–March 1900].)

FRANK G. SPECK, "Ceremonial Songs of the Creek and Yuchi Indians," *University of Pennsylvania Museum Anthropological Papers* 1, no. 2 (1911).

Speck writes, "Translations such as these were offered by Kibitcimala when the texts were being recorded. As they were almost incapable of analysis and unintelligible to other interpreters, evidently the informant himself was the only one who could understand them."

"**Creek Drunken Dance**" is a Dance Song from the Creeks of Taskigi town, one of the subdivisions of the Creek Nation. It was sung by Kibitcimala (Raccoon Leader), a prominent shaman. In this "pleasure dance," the men and women followed the leader around the fire, those who were not drunk acting as if they were. The leader impersonated the man and the woman, and then the voice of the outsider at the end.

MAURICE BOYD, *Kiowa Voices, vol. 1: Ceremonial Dance, Ritual, and Song,* ed. Donald Worcester (Texas Christian University Press, 1981).

"**Warpath Song**" is part of a Mourning Dance. The girl had been preparing for the successful return of a war party, but instead the leader gave the signal of death. **"Lullaby"** is "so old that its origin has been lost in antiquity," says Boyd.

DAVID P. McALLESTER, *Peyote Music*, Viking Fund Publications in Anthropology, no. 13 (1949).

Published peyote songs are very few. These were collected in 1940 in Indiahoma, Oklahoma. The "peyote cult" is a nightlong ceremony of the Native American Church. A drum and rattle are passed clockwise (sunwise) and when a member receives the rattle he sings some songs, usually four, then passes it on. The drum follows, so each man drums for the man next to him.

Comanche peyote ceremonies are held either for curing or when people have the desire to sponsor gatherings in the special tipi. Women attend but do not participate very actively. Singing goes on until about midnight, and then peyote buttons are consumed.

Each "line" of "Comanche Peyote Songs" is part of a separate song that McAllester collected. It should be noted that I am only using the lexical text of each song. This is not one long peyote song but a series of translatable fragments, each of which is embedded in vocables that often constitute the major part of the text. The singer Tekwakï collected the songs into groups of four (a system that cannot be duplicated here since sometimes the words are in Apache, and Comanche informants could not translate them; sometimes only vocables are used). He sang thirteen sets or groups of four together, adding or dropping songs as he saw fit. Tekwakï composed most of the songs, though he also borrowed. In the old days, he said, "the songs were sung in a sort of story system," and one can still see a sort of rough grouping. There are, for example, the three songs referring to the eagle and hell-diver (anhinga), sacred to peyote. Still, as McAllester notes, "in a good many of the song groups the relationship of ideas expressed seems somewhat remote." Another idea that permeates is dawn, the time when the ceremony is coming to an end and people are tired. At dawn (and midnight) there is an elaborate ritual connected with a woman bringing water into the tipi. Song 56 (seventeen lines from the end of my version) tells the woman to go for water near the end of the ceremony. Peyote itself is the "red flower" associated with power, daylight, and the sun; it comes "from the south." Peyote equipment referred to includes "tipi poles," "cane brace," and "reed whistle." "What are you holding? A dove?" questions the propriety of the dove fan one of the members is holding. "The wooden object" is a bull-roarer, which is used in other ceremonies but not in this. Its mention here is meant to evoke other healing ceremonies.

Other song references remain enigmatic or even private—songs are sometimes obtained with the help of peyote in visions. ("I was talking. I began to talk about the cane brace. I was talking to someone who was to come. I ate peyote. It made me feel good, the power of peyote seemed to lay the song in front of me. I do not know the reason why I put 'brace' in"—Tekwakï.) The last song was obtained from another Comanche who had heard a coyote at dawn telling him coyotes were his friends and "anything you do on earth, you shall not go wrong."

FRANCIS LA FLESCHE, *The Osage Tribe: Part 1, Rite of the Chiefs, Sayings of the Ancient Men,* 36th Annual Report of the Bureau of American Ethnology, 1914–15, Smithsonian Institution (Washington, D.C., 1918).

The original home of the Osage was along the Osage River in Missouri. They moved from their reservation in Kansas in 1872 to Osage County, Oklahoma, at a time when sudden oil wealth had led to the rapid dying of ceremonial life. It was then that La Flesche worked with them.

The tribe was divided into two, one symbolizing sky, the other earth. For ceremonial purposes they were further divided into gentes and subgentes, each with its own mythical life-story, functions, and so on. From the initiatory ceremony called Wa-the'-the, "The Sending," I have drawn examples of intoned or recited songs. (The Sending refers to "the sending to the various gentes of the two great tribal divisions the life symbols belonging to each.") La Flesche notes that members of each gens recite simultaneously, but not in unison, the words that tell the meaning of its own life symbols. "The result is a confused sound of words, and the sight is expressive of individual devotion to the task at hand."

The Puma is the life symbol of the Puma gens of the Honga great tribal division. The animal is closely associated with the sun, the great life symbol. Charcoal is emblematic of its fire. "**The Puma**" recitation continues from where I have left off, with Puma providing more symbols for the gens: roots, beans, turkeys, and others.

Francis La Flesche was the first Native American anthropologist. His father, Joseph La Flesche, was one of the principal chiefs of the

Omaha at the time of the 1854 treaty. He was half French, son of a fur trader, and half Ponca (his mother grew up among the Omahas). Francis La Flesche's mother, Tainne, was full-blood Omaha.

Anthropologist Hartley B. Alexander has called the four-volume *The Osage Tribe*, the work of nineteen years, "the most complete single record of the ceremonies of a North American Indian people," and Joan Mark dubs it "a monument of American Indian scholarship." (Both quotes are from Joan Mark, *A Stranger in Her Native Land: Alice Fletcher and the American Indians* [University of Nebraska Press, 1988]; this book also discusses in detail the longtime relationship between La Flesche and Fletcher.)

ALICE C. FLETCHER AND FRANCIS LA FLESCHE, A *Study of Omaha Indian Music*, Archeological and Ethnological Papers of the Peabody Museum, vol. 1, no. 5 (1893).

Men in a war party, or scouts, described themselves as "wolves." Wolf songs were sung as men left the village or when traveling and in no immediate danger. **"Wolf Song"** was sung by a war-party leader when he had been away a long time and the men were homesick. Fletcher supplies the following: "wa-oo, women; ah-ma, they; wae-tha-he-ba, have gone for wood; hoo-zha-wa, are happy; hte, really or very; ma-thin-ah, mah-in-tae, they must be walking; thae-thu, here; wakh-pa-thin, very poor; hte, very; mum-b'thin-hae, I walk," and translates the song as "the women have gone to gather wood and are having a joyous time chattering amid the trees while here very miserable am I walking."

J. OWEN DORSEY, "Omaha Songs," *Journal of American Folklore* 1, no. 1 (April–June 1888).

"Waganca's Song" was sung from the woman's viewpoint. Dorsey notes that "as he wished to marry her, he does not mention her name."

GERTRUDE P. KURATH, "Antiphonal Songs of the Eastern Woodland Indians," *Musical Quarterly* 42, no. 4 (October 1956).

The **"Iroquois Trotting Dance Song"** was sung by Huron Miller of the Six Nations Reserve in Ontario. The Trotting Dance is a social dance.

FRANK G. SPECK, *Penobscot Man* (Octagon Books, New York, 1976; originally published in 1940).

The Penobscot live in northern Maine, where these songs were collected on a phonograph during 1907 and 1908. They were transcribed by J. D. Sapir. **"The Deserted Woman"** (my title) is a myth song, "an example of music to which myths were sung," in this case the popular story of a deserted woman. Song myths are not straightforward narratives but, says Speck, "disconnected ideas and expressions relevant to the subject, intelligible enough to those who knew the story, but incoherent to others." Speck is witness to changing mores with **"Woman's Song"**: "While there attaches an obscene side to it now, they claim that formerly it was a 'perfectly proper song,' a sort of ballad." Such songs are improvised.

CORA DU BOIS, "The 1870 Ghost Dance," *University of California Publications in Anthropological Records* 3, no. 1 (1939-46).

Between 1875 and 1895, the Wintu of northern California had their own cult, the Dream Dance, an outgrowth of the Earth Lodge Cult, unconnected with the Ghost Dance. (The Ghost Dance had stressed the return of the dead; the Earth Lodge Cult emphasized the end of the world. The Earth Lodge would protect the faithful.) The dreaming of songs was an integral part of this cult, though the common belief was that people who dreamed songs wouldn't live long. The subject of these songs was *olel* ("above," heaven) and *luli* (flower). The interest was in life after death, at a time when the Indians of northern California were under stress from white invasion. (For other songs of the Dream Dance see D. Demetracopoulou, *Anthropos* 30 [1935], which I adapted in *Song of the Sky*.)

Song I of **Wintu Dream Dance Songs** was sung by Harry Marsh, while the singer of Song II is unknown (the original has "minnow maiden" for "minnow," but with no explanation; perhaps the minnow maiden is a figure of myth). Song III was sung by Sadie Marsh (the song was given in a dream by a friend who had just died). Song IV, a shaman song and a favorite at funerals, was sung by Jim Thomas— the Marshes and Thomas were also Demetracopoulou's sources.

The Dream Dance ceremonies centered around the songs. The women held handkerchiefs and flowers in their hands or put them on their heads, with feathers. They painted red stripes on their faces. The men wore feather skirts and painted their chests with two black stripes from shoulder to shoulder. They danced indoors or in a circular brush enclosure to drums, rattles, and whistles. Sick people also danced, since the ceremony was used to cure.

RICHARD KEELING, "Contrast of Song Performance Style as a Function of Sex Role Polarity in the Hupa Brush Dance," *Ethnomusicology* 29, no. 2 (spring/summer 1985).

"**Hupa Love Song,**" originally titled "Light Song," was sung by Herman Sherman, Sr., and addressed by an older man to the sweetheart of his youth. Songs in the Brush Dance are short and are sung three times, all through the night. There are "heavy" songs and "light" songs. Heavy songs are sung by a man, after which other men and girls perform light songs, many of which are composed of vocables.

Among the Hupa of northern California, the Brush Dance was a curing ritual dance for moody or sickly children or for someone who had violated a taboo, usually sexual. During the winter Brush Dance season the sexes slept apart. When it was over it was time for flirting and romance. Today, the curing ritual is largely symbolic, but the ritual is enacted much as before. In the center of the Brush Dance pit, a medicine woman and her helper work on the baby— hold it in the steam of certain herbs, massage it, wave burning pitchwood sticks over it—while younger girls file in and sing to help lift the spiritual penalty from the child. For more on California music see Keeling's "Music and Culture History Among the Yurok and Neighboring Tribes of Northwestern California," *Journal of Anthropological Research* 48, no. 1 (spring 1992), 25–48, and his book *Cry for Luck: Sacred Song and Speech among the Yurok, Hupa, and Karok Indians of Northwestern California* (University of California Press, 1992).

A. L. KROEBER, *The Yokuts Language of South Central California*, University of California Publications in American Archeology and Ethnology, vol. 2, no. 1 (1904-7).

Kroeber uses the texts as linguistic and grammatic illustrations, or data; he didn't do the usual "free versions," just word-by-word literal ones, and gave few hints as to meaning. My version of "**Coyote's Song**" is rather free. Here is Kroeber's literal translation: "Coyote said what-am I? Coyote I well, water-in I what am I Coyote I." There is no explanation of "water-in I," so I had to omit it, though it seems to refer to a myth incident. For Coyote see William Bright, *A Coyote Reader* (University of California Press, 1993). The song I have called "**Song of the Eclipse**" Kroeber described as "sung, accompanied by dancing, by an old woman at an eclipse of the sun."

A. L. KROEBER, *Handbook of the Indians of California*, Smithsonian Institution, Bureau of American Ethnology, Bulletin no. 78 (Washington, D.C., 1919).

This "intoned prayer" is from the Yauelmani, a southern Yokuts group from the San Joaquin Valley. It is addressed to the seven gods of the Yokuts and recited not so much for any specific wish "as for the general fulfillments of good fortune."

CONSTANCE GODDARD DU BOIS, *The Religion of the Luiseño Indians of Southern California*, University of California Publications in American Archeology and Ethnology, vol. 8, no. 3 (1908–10).

These songs were collected in San Diego County in 1906. The Luiseño, of the Uto-Aztecan language family, and the Diegueño, of the Yuman family, were formerly attached to Franciscan missions (the Luiseño were attached to San Luis Rey). These three songs are Songs of Temenganesh, Songs of Seasons, part of the Image ceremony, which includes the Pikmakvul series, Songs of Death, and the Nokwanish, Songs in Memory of the Dead (which I used in *Song of the Sky*, basing my versions on Helen H. Roberts' *Form in Primitive Music* [1933]; she had the words as "Pimukval" and "Nokwa'nik").

Song I was sung by Albanas, as were the others. The butterfly's house is a *pohota*, a circular enclosure made of brush in which religious ceremonies are held. The chipmunk and squirrel have a *marakul*, a log hollowed out and used for holding acorns, a staple of diet. The allusion is to a myth in which Chipmunk, when he was one of the First People, carried a log ten men could not lift. Du Bois gives the last line as "it is time for the acorns to fall from the trees." But, since the song refers to spring, I changed it slightly.

In Song II, "bison" is *uchanut*, "a fabulous animal, identified with the bison." "In the south other animals give birth" is the best I could do, since Du Bois simply gives two Luiseño animal names without translating them.

In Song III, the stick used to beat Coyote is from a Creation myth, and the "ringing stones" are used in the girls' puberty ritual.

HELEN H. ROBERTS, *Form in Primitive Music: An Analytical and Comparative Study of the Melodic Forms of Some Ancient Southern California Indian Songs* (W. W. Norton & Co., 1933).

Sung by Luiseño Celestino Awaiu of Pichanga, this is a *senyam* song—Senyam was the name of the tribe that came from the ocean, from Catalina, and stayed around what is now San Luis Rey. After they were there awhile, the wild geese came and set down there, and the people thought this was a good sign. They farmed, and everything grew the first season. Then the gulls came, and that was another good sign. Finally, the bees came, and after that they claimed a good living was assured. **"Senyam Planting Song"** is a commemoration of those times and may be of the type called "monivul," "songs of travel of journeying," which relate the wanderings of the people after they emerged from the underground darkness where they were born and began looking for places to live on earth. These songs constitute rights to certain lands; the ability to sing them was proof of those rights.

A. WATERMAN, *The Religious Practices of the Diegueño Indians*, University of California Publications in American Archeology and Ethnology, vol. 8, no. 4 (1910).

"The Eagle Ceremony," or Dance, was a mourning ceremony held on the anniversary of the death of a *kwaipai*, or leader of the dance. It was held at the end of a three-day festival. Toward nightfall, the old men danced for two or three hours; then speeches began, explaining that the old men had decided to get together clothes and property to send to the *kwaipai*, and kill the eagle to send with messages to him. The eagle was killed by pointing at it with a stick (in fact its heart was crushed surreptitiously by the person holding it). The next day, the eagle was buried to weeping ("it is done"). I have run together the various songs for, as Waterman says, "The reader can see that the songs seem to outline a myth or story." References to myth include the friendship of Eagle and Chicken Hawk.

HERBERT J. SPINDEN, *Songs of the Tewa* (Exposition of Indian Tribal Arts, New York, 1933).

Public interest in Native American arts (especially those of the Southwest) was high in the 1920s and 1930s, despite continuing efforts to suppress "pagan" ceremonies. In 1931, the Exposition of Indian Tribal Arts was held on Madison Avenue in New York City, and for the first time these arts were described as "art" and not "ethnology." A feature of the exposition was a series of pamphlets on American Indian life, and *Songs of the Tewa* had its origin here.

Spinden doesn't cite singer, ceremony, or provenance for "**Song of the Sky Loom**," though it is placed between others from Nambe and San Juan, two of the six Tewa villages north of Sante Fe; the others are San Ildefonso, Santa Clara, Pojoaque, and Tesuque. For a detailed discussion of the Tewa, especially of the author's native San Juan, see Alfonso Ortiz, *The Tewa World: Space, Time, Being, and Becoming in a Pueblo Society* (University of Chicago Press, 1969). In a note, Spinden says the sky loom refers to small desert rains that resemble a loom hung from the sky, and "the symbolic decoration on the white cotton mantle, once the regular dress but now put to ceremonial use, is in accordance with this chant or prayer for well-being."

In a review of the third printing of *Songs of the Tewa* by Sunstone Press of Santa Fe in 1993, the Tewa reviewer Tito Naranjo says that "the song and its poetic words best illustrate the traditional Tewa person's daily philosophy and quest, *'gi woatsi tuenji,'* or 'we are seeking life.'" He praises Spinden for saving songs and "priceless sacred ceremonies" and notes that the book is especially useful "for educated Tewa readers curious about recordings of songs when great-grandfather spoke only Tewa" (*American Indian Quarterly*, summer 1994, p. 426).

LINDA J. GOODMAN, "The Form and Function of the Basket Dance of San Juan Pueblo" (MA thesis, Wesleyan University, May 1968).

The Basket Dance is performed at the end of January or beginning of February, "to seek life for the good of all." The elaborate preparations include four nights' practice in a kiva. Prayers before the practice recount the reasons for doing the dance and offer words of encouragement to the performers: "The people want to be liked, to be loved, they want moisture, and they want good crops," as Goodman was told.

In the "**Prelude Dance**," the line of male dancers dances in place, the whole line rotating 180 degrees at appropriate times. In the "**Slow Standing Dance**," both male and female lines rotate together 180 degrees, east and west. (Note that in this dance "corn flowers" are the tassels on the corn plants.) In the "**Fast Kneeling Dance**," male and female dancers face each other in line. The women kneel and rub their scraping sticks together. The men dance where they stand. There are ten dances in all.

The Prelude Dance song was composed about 1933 by Eliseo

Montoya, uncle of the singer Steve Trujillo. The Slow Standing Dance song was composed by Kaats'aa Garcia, father of the singer David Garcia. The Fast Kneeling Dance song was composed in 1942 by Juanito Trujillo and sung by Steve Trujillo. The songs must be sung correctly for the desired results. Certain families are singing families; women are of secondary importance as musicians and do not compose songs.

The Basket Dance gets its name because the women carry a basket in their right hand. In the Fast Kneeling Dance, women kneel facing the men and turn their baskets upside down. One notched stick is placed against the top of the basket and the woman rubs it with the other, producing a grating sound. The baskets symbolize food—in the year's round, seeds will be first in the baskets, then corn, meal, bread. Rubbing sticks symbolizes grinding.

The whole dance and song structure is symbolic, reflecting the dual division of Tewa society, as well as the sacred numbers 4 and 6 (cardinal directions plus up and down). I have not attempted to duplicate this.

Pueblo musical style is highly complex. For a detailed description, including a section on the present status of Rio Grande Pueblo music and dance, see "The Ethnomusicology of the Eastern Pueblos" by Don L. Roberts, in Alfonso Ortiz, ed., *New Perspectives on the Pueblos* (University of New Mexico Press, 1972). For more on the San Juan Tunshare, or Basket Dance, see Gertrude Kurath and Antonio Garcia's *Music and Dance of the Tewa Pueblos* (cited in the next note). The best book on the structure of the Tewa universe is Alfonso Ortiz, *The Tewa World* (see preceding note). The best book on Pueblo culture is Edward P. Dozier's *The Pueblo Indians of North America* (Holt, Rinehart & Winston, 1970).

I would like to thank Linda Goodman and Peter Garcia, not only for permission to use these materials but for corrections and help.

GERTRUDE P. KURATH AND ANTONIO GARCIA, *Music and Dance of the Tewa Pueblos* (Museum of New Mexico Press, 1970).

These songs were collected from 1957 to 1965. The Tembishare or Harvest Dance is held every four or five years in the Tewa pueblos of San Juan, San Ildefonso, Santa Clara, Tesuque, and Nambe. To the **"Tewa Entrance Song,"** people dance in a meandering line into the plaza. The order of file is:

1. Kosa Society, heads, and assistants (ceremonial clowns of the winter moiety)
2. Summer cacique with assistants
3. Winter cacique with assistants
4. Bear Society priest and assistants
5. Kwirana Society (ceremonial clowns of the summer moiety)
6. Game priest
7. Governor, civil officers, war chief, assistants
8. Women's Society
9. Scalp Society priest (obsolete, so not recorded)
10. Summer moiety representatives
11. Winter moiety representatives

At the first station, in a circle, gifts are thrown into the middle for spectators. The dancers move sideways, clockwise, to the drumbeat. Each group is represented by its own special song. When this group is featured, the dancer enters the center of the circle and he and his assistants form a line. They face one way and then its opposite (e.g., north, then south). Outside, the dancers go sideways, swinging their arms, palms facing down. In the center, the dancers turn left and right in a small arc, palms forward—perhaps, says Kurath, to invoke earth and sky. The songs contain vocables and repetitions, and each song is sometimes sung four times.

In number 10, "Shiwana" are rain gods (compare the line in the poem "Dry Root in a Wash" by Simon Ortiz of Acoma Pueblo: "Upstream, toward the mountain, / the Shiwana work for rain"). Also in number 10 I have used "oxua boys" as a variation (supplied by Kurath) on "Cloud Rain Gods."

"One-Eyed Ford" is from Appendix 4, "Tewa Pueblo Round Dances," by Don L. Roberts. Round Dances are very popular and widespread social dances known by a variety of names, mostly performed after ceremonial dances or on separate occasions. Dancers form a circle around the singer, holding hands. They lock arms and circle, usually clockwise, with short bouncing side steps. Formerly they were meeting places for the sexes but increasingly "American" dances are taking over that function; Round Dances acquired a "questionable reputation" among some tribes, including the Cheyenne, because of the dancers' "promiscuous behavior" (see Virginia Giglio, *Southern Cheyenne Women's Songs* [University of Oklahoma Press, 1994]). But Round Dances are still popular at powwows.

Round Dances are also known as "Forty-nine" dances—the name is from traveling carnivals in Oklahoma, which included a sideshow called "Days of 'Forty-nine," a dance hall with decor from the California gold-rush era. There was an admission charge to dance with showgirls. Young Indians decided to set up their own " 'Forty-nine." It is fairly certain that the dance originated with the Kiowa or Comanche in Oklahoma, 1911–18, and spread rapidly. (In Kiowa culture, "Forty-niner" songs have replaced the old tribal War Departure or Travel Songs, and the same happened with the Southern Cheyenne where war journey songs, Wolf Songs, and songs from other tribes evolved into the Forty-nine repertory.) For more on this topic, see Norman Feder, "Origin of the Oklahoma Forty-nine Dance," *Ethnomusicology* 8, no. 3 (September 1964). This Forty-nine song, "a popular number on the Round Dance Hit Parade," according to Feder, is from San Juan Pueblo.

Songs are humorous or serious and are often sung in English. Contemporary Native American poets draw on the Forty-nine tradition. Diane Burns (Anishinabe/Chemehueve), for instance, named her first book of poetry *Riding the One-Eyed Ford* (1981), and Paiute Adrian C. Louis explained how the Ford earned its sobriquet in "This Is the Rez" (*Exquisite Corpse*, no. 48 [1994]):

> "This is the rez.
> Many times the luminous legions
> of night-driving cars
> will have only one headlight.
> They are the notorious 'one-eyed Fords.' "

RUTH L. BUNZEL, *Zuñi Ritual Poetry*, Fourth Annual Report of the Bureau of American Ethnology, 1929–30, Smithsonian Institution (Washington, D.C., 1932).

"Sayateca's Morning Chant" can be thought of as a companion piece to "Sayateca's Night Chant," part of which I used in *Song of the Sky*, and which Andrew Wiget translated and discussed in *American Indian Culture and Research Journal* 4, nos. 1–2 (1980). It is part of the extensive Ha'lako (Shalako) ceremony, "Prayers and Chants of the Priests of the Masked Gods." The Ha'lako are kachinas, and kachinas are intermediaries between the Zuni and a higher order of spirits. Sayateca represents fertility and ancestral water spirits through whom he will bring prosperity to the people. The Masked God, the kachina Sayateca, has great dignity and prestige; "his voice booms with authority and importance," Bunzel notes. The prayers are highly formal in content and expression.

This ceremony closes the Zuni year at the winter solstice. At the first sign of dawn, Sayateca goes to the roof and unties the last knot in the counting string. He chants this morning prayer, stretching out the string at the end of each line. The prayer is afterward repeated in the house.

"Plume wands" are sacred prayer sticks made for all Sayateca's party by the priests, the men of the house, and their close relatives. "My children" refers to the other Ha'lako impersonators. The "mothers" exhausted by the fireplace are the women who cook the feast. The prayer meal is used to sprinkle the gods during the progress around the village in the afternoon of their entrance. "The song cycles of our fathers" refers to the choir of the medicine society that sang for them. "Pekwin" is a priest (also called "rain-bringing bird"). "Ayayaka" (Ayayakakwi), "bluebird place," is one of twenty-eight sacred springs visited by ancestors of the Zuni, and still visited by the Zuni, in their migration from Emergence Place; springs are doorways of the rainmakers (the kachinas live in a sacred village at the bottom of wells). "Mist" is wordplay; the Zuni are masters of wordplay and multivalencies of meaning, as Bunzel points out and Andrew Wiget discusses what he calls the "superior verbal creation" in the essay cited earlier. (M. Jane Young's "Ethnopoetic Retranslation of a Zuni Ritual Song Sequence," in Brian Swann, ed., *Coming to Light: Contemporary Translations of the Native Literatures of North America* [Random House, 1995], is very useful in this regard; see also Barbara Tedlock's essay "Songs of the Zuni Kachina Society: Composition, Rehearsal, and Performance" in Charlotte J. Frisbie, ed., *Southwestern Indian Ritual Drama* [University of New Mexico Press, 1980].)

"Cipololon.e" means both "mist" and "ceremonial smoke" and points up the fertility aspect of the ritual. To "add to the hearts" is a common phrase for offerings to the supernaturals. The "clothing bundle" is not ordinary clothing but any movable wealth. The "roads" refer to the lines of prayer meal drawn on the ground. The "water-filled woodpile" refers not only to a special woodpile, made by laying short sticks over two long poles, but to the kiva ladder by which Sayateca enters, and the bundle of prayer sticks arranged in terraced form, as well as to the steps by which the rain gods descend from above. It would be impossible to elucidate here all the rich layered ceremonial language, the poetry.

Ruth Bunzel was one of Franz Boas' graduate students. Ruth Benedict was her teacher and co-worker at Zuni. For more on both women, as well as on modernism and anthropology, see Margaret M. Caffrey, *Ruth Benedict: Stranger in This Land* (University of Texas Press, 1989).

BARBARA TEDLOCK, "Songs of the Zuni Kachina Society: Composition, Rehearsal, and Performance," in Charlotte J. Frisbie, ed., *Southwestern Indian Ritual Drama* (University of New Mexico Press, 1980).

Each kiva group in the kachina society usually has song composers in its membership. "Zuni composers feel that good text composition within the kachina call genre consists of what sounds like the usual lyrics about rain and other blessings, which are often lines from prayers, but it is 'really about some other something today, right now,'" writes Tedlock. So, during the summer of 1972, one of the Small Group composers composed **"They Went to the Moon Mother"** in the genre "Downy Feather on a String," an allegory about two stars (two astronauts) who went to the Moon Mother on a dragonfly (a rocket ship). They report to the people via the sacred bundle (Houston Control) that the moon will bless them with silt (alluvial deposits believed to be on the moon, and in the Southwest after heavy rain). The "stretching" refers to the corn plants reaching out for rain, the people reaching old age, and the rocket reaching the moon.

The first part, the "coming out" section, as Tedlock terms it, using Zuni terminology, has the astronauts talking, and in the third part, the "talking about" section, the "masker" is speaking, but it is not clear to me who is speaking the second or "strong" section.

GEORGE LIST, *Stability and Variation in Hopi Song*, American Philosophical Society, Memoirs Series, vol. 204 (Philadelphia, 1893).

A kachina is a masked male impersonator of spiritual beings who come to villages to assist in securing rain and fertility of the land. **"Hopi Barefoot Kachina Dance Song"** is a composite text from First and Third Mesas; it is spoken, not sung.

Starting in December, each kiva performs a kachina dance in the kiva for four consecutive weekends. In summer, some dances are repeated in the plaza. There are two types of longhaired kachinas, the one who wears shoes and the one who goes barefoot: the *angak-china* and the *katoch-ang-ak-china*. For an analysis of one of these songs, see David Leedom Shaul's "A Hopi Song-Poem in 'Context'" in Brian Swann, ed., *On the Translation of Native American Literatures*, as well as his "Two Hopi Songpoems" in Swann, ed., *Coming to Light*.

H. R. VOTH, *The Traditions of the Hopi*, Field Columbian Museum Publication 96, Anthropological Series, vol. 8 (Chicago, 1905).

Many of the stories in Voth's volume contain songs. I've selected **"Song of the Locusts"** from "The Snakes and the Locusts," in which the Snakes are suffering from cold and snow. They go to the Locusts, who live in a pleasant climate and always seem to be warm, and beg them to warm things up. The Locusts agree and start "chirping through the flutes," so the Snakes have an easy road home through the melting snow. By the time they get home, spring has arrived. The Locusts follow, and as soon as they enter the Snake kiva they line up and sing this song, "dancing while singing and shaking small rattles."

White Earth Locust Youth refers to one of the two divisions of the Locusts, the Dumámahu (White Earth or Kaolin Máhu). The other division is simply the Máhu (Locusts). "My fathers, my mothers" is honorific.

JESSE WALTER FEWKES, *Hopi Katcina Songs*, ed. Charles Hofmann, Folkways Records, album no. FE 4394 (1964).

These songs were collected in Arizona in 1924. **"Hopi Eagle Dance,"** side 2, band 5, was performed by two young men side by side. It can be held any time, preceded by a four-day fast, during which the sick are treated in the kiva.

In the 1890s, Fewkes (and others) described Hopi Clown Songs. For a recent account of this continuing tradition see Hans-Ulrich Sanner, "'Another Home Run for the Black Sox': Humor and Creativity in Hopi Ritual Clown Songs," in Arnold Krupat, ed., *New Voices in Native American Literary Criticism* (Smithsonian Institution Press, 1993), 149–173.

A. M. STEPHENS, *Hopi Journal* (Columbia University Press, 1936); in "The Indian Music Program Performance Series: Hopi and Apache Music," Museum of Indian Arts and Culture, Santa Fe, New Mexico, September 17, 1988, program notes by Linda J. Goodman, Lawrence and Griselda Saufkie, and Nathaniel Chee.

The **"Hopi Butterfly Dance Song"** is a social dance performed in August and early September, "when many butterflies are in the fields and are viewed as an attractive and important part of the continuation of life," says Stephens. The dance is performed when some of the corn is ready for picking and is the occasion for a feast. Boys and girls dance. Often seven dance sets are performed for two days. The dance is sometimes a counterclockwise circuit and sometimes two lines facing. The dancers enter and exit from the east. This is just one of a number of songs.

WASHINGTON MATTHEWS, "Songs of the Navajo," *Land of Sunshine* 5 (1896).
The Mountain Chant is a nine-day ceremony. Matthews uses this song as an example of antithesis, "a favorite figure with the Navajo poet." Others have used **"Song from the Mountain Chant"** to point out the unity of the Navajo universe.

WASHINGTON MATTHEWS, comp. and trans., *Navajo Legends*, Memoirs of the American Folk-Lore Society, vol. 5 (1897; new edition, foreword by Grace A. McNeley, University of Utah Press, 1994).
The Night Chant is a great healing ceremony, "the most popular ceremony" according to Matthews, and consists of twenty-four sequences and a total of 324 songs (it must be performed only in late fall and winter). The first four days are devoted largely to purification and evocation, the next four to rituals of identification and transformation, and the last, the ninth night, summarizes and releases the patient. The **"Prayer of the First Dancers"** (*Atsálei*) is spoken at the beginning of the last night by the spiritual practitioner, with the patient repeating it. The performers are four *yébaka*, or male divinities, and Hastséyalti, the Talking God or *Yébitsai*. The first *yébaka* is "genius" of the corn, the second "chief of the rain child," the third chief of all plants, and the fourth chief of the pollen. They are also spoken of as thunderbirds, and as having the colors of the four cardinal points. For more on the Night Chant, see Washington Matthews, *The Night Chant: A Navajo Ceremony*, Memoirs of the American Museum of Natural History, 6 (May 1902), and "A Tale of Kininaékai: Accounting for the Origin of Certain Prayers and Songs of the Night Chant," *University of California Publications in American Archeology and Ethnology* 5, no. 2 (1907–10).
Tsegíhi (White House) is where the gods (*yei*) live. The prayer is

addressed to a thunderbird, a male divinity who lives at Tsegíhi. "Male rain" is, Matthews explains, a "shower accompanied by thunder and lightning," "female rain" is a "shower without electric display." The "smoke" that is prepared is painted reed cigarettes filled with native tobacco and sealed with moistened pollen. The cigarettes are placed in the patient's hands. As for the spell, the deity, being capable of good and evil, would seem to have had something to do with it in the first place, and so he can lift it.

The key word here, as elsewhere in Navajo ceremony, is *hozó* (or *Hózhǫ́*). Matthews says it means "primarily, earthly beauty"; one of its derivatives, *hozógo*, means "beautiful on the earth," while another, *hozóna*, signifies "again beautiful," and so on—he translates such terms as "happily," "in beauty," and in other ways since "they must be rendered by various English words." Gary Witherspoon, however, a leading scholar of Navajo, in his *Language and Art in the Navajo Universe* (University of Michigan Press, 1977), translates *Hózhǫ́* as "a beautiful, pleasant, and healthy environment," "the positive or ideal environment," and says it is "the central idea in Navajo religious thinking." The Navajo uses this concept "to express his happiness, his health, the beauty of his land, and the harmony of his relations with others." When a Navajo says good-bye to someone leaving, he or she says, "*hózhóogo naninaadoo*," "May you walk or go about according to *Hózhǫ́*" (compare "walk in beauty"). In my version, I have retained the familiar "in beauty" most of the time because it is, if looked at clearly, a concept that makes us pay special attention. If everything is "in beauty" it is harmonious to our mind and senses. However, toward the end, "happily," which translates *hozógo*, is not very good, based, as it is, on "hap" or "chance." *Hózhǫ́* and its derivative *hozógo* are not the result of accident, but effort and perception. It is interesting to note that the Night Chant has provided titles for two important books: N. Scott Momaday's Pulitzer Prize–winning novel of 1968, *House Made of Dawn* (it also provided an important part of the structure and theme), and George W. Cronyn's pioneering anthology of Native American literature, *The Path on the Rainbow* (1918).

In her useful foreword to the new edition of the Night Chant, Grace McNeley calls Matthews' work "the root and trunk of the tree of knowledge about Navajo life," from which all later scholars drew sustenance. Matthews was born in Ireland and came to this country at age four. He obtained a medical degree from the University of

Iowa in 1864. The Night Chant brought him fame as the author of the first complete description of an Indian ceremony. McNeley notes that Matthews wanted to salvage the ceremonies, but, "in retrospect, Navajo culture of a hundred years ago did not need to be salvaged by outsiders. Long before, the Navajo Nation had developed its own ways of preserving its sacred and cultural knowledge. The work of Matthews is now being utilized in ways he could scarcely have imagined, not only by *bilagaana* [white] scholars in their continuing efforts to comprehend an 'alien' living culture, but also by modern Navajo as a secondary source of knowledge to supplement that of their fathers and grandfathers."

WASHINGTON MATTHEWS, *The Mountain Chant: A Navajo Ceremony*, Fifth Annual Report of the Bureau of American Ethnology 1883–84, Smithsonian Institution (Washington, D.C., 1887).

"**First Song of the Thunder**" and "**Twelfth Song of the Thunder**," like the Night Chant, are widely anthologized. They are from the public ceremonies on the last of nine nights, after the private ceremonies of the days before. The purpose of the ceremony is curative, invoking unseen powers. The majority of Navajo ceremonies are held in winter. This is no exception. "Mountain Chant" is literally "chant towards (a place) within the mountains," and it is understood as a reference to a myth where the originator of these ceremonies ("the prophet") lived.

In "**Fifth Daylight Song**," Daylight Boy (or Dawn Boy) is the Navajo dawn god. Daylight Girl is the dawn goddess.

KARL W. LUCKERT, *The Navajo Hunter Tradition* (University of Arizona Press, 1975).

"**The Making of the Game Animals**" is from the manuscript of Father Berard Haile (1874–1961). The material was obtained and translated from the version of James Smith, a policeman at Chinle.

Game was made at "Stretchable House," the house (hogan) of First Man. The game creators included Talking God, Dawn People, Calling God and the Holy People of "the horizontal blue," Black God, and Begochidi. (For a work of related interest see Luckert's *Coyoteway: A Navajo Holyway Healing Ceremonial* [University of Arizona Press, 1979].)

The stress on *thinking* as the means of creation is typically Navajo for, as Gary Witherspoon has pointed out in *Language and Art in the Navajo Universe* (University of Michigan Press, 1977), the "Navajo interpretation of the constitution of reality and the causation of events are all based on an unbreakable connection between mind and matter. In this regard, primary importance and creative power is always attributed to thought and speech." The *Diyin Dine'e* (gods) thought the world into existence. These thoughts were realized through speech, song, and prayer.

LELAND C. WYMAN, *Blessingway* (University of Arizona Press, 1970). All the Blessingway material was gathered by Father Berard Haile from Slim Curly of Crystal, New Mexico, in 1932, Frank Mitchell of Chinle, Arizona, and River Junction Curly, also of Chinle. All the songs here are from Slim Curly's version.

Wyman notes that the purpose of Blessingway is to vitalize and personalize each phenomenon. "By themselves," he says, "natural phenomena are lifeless, but an inner human form set within them functions as the life principle." Blessingway, which usually lasts two nights, is used to invoke blessings on the totality of human life. It is a "total" ceremony, deeply concerned with the hogan, "the home place," the center of every blessing, representative of the cosmos. All Blessingway ceremonies begin with hogan songs, which originated with First Man, who had knowledge of all things, in the first hogan. These songs dedicate the hogan to religious purposes.

Chief Hogan Songs describe the plan for the hogan. The planner is the head man (as First Man was the first planner), and the songs originated in the first hogan, where plans were made for endowing natural phenomena with inner forms. The hogan is serenaded as "hogan woman," where beauty radiates from inner spaces.

In the first song, "my hogan's stones are set" refers to the two stones embedded in the ground next to the east pole. Two posts are set on these to receive the entrance curtain. The stones are symbolic of the fact that the hogan and its songs continue on after wood has decayed. "I'm the one who knows" refers to the fact that the head man knows which materials are suitable, where to get each item, how to set and arrange them, and all the other details.

"How Changing Woman Was Picked Up" is the first of ten songs epitomizing the story of the birth of Changing Woman (who might be thought of as the Earth herself). For Haile's "Corn Beetle" I would have substituted "the Ripener," in line with David McAllester's practice, but it sounded a bit too abstract. McAllester points out that "the Ripener" more closely translates the Navajo *Anlt'anii*, "a god associated with the ripening of the corn, and often paired with Pollen Boy. It has been referred to as a 'grasshopper,' 'corn bug,' and, most often, 'corn-beetle' in the literature" (*Hogans: Navajo Houses and House Songs* [Wesleyan University Press, 1980], 88).

After the inner forms of the sacred mountains have been created, and the songs sung, comes "Dawn Song." Boy-who-returns-with-single-turquoise is the son of Dawn Woman, and his father is the Sun.

Long Mustache told Haile that "Blessingway is representative for them [the other chantways], it is the spinal column of songs." It is not part of the curative chantways, but central to them in theme and ceremony, though no sandpaintings are used. Instead, Blessingway paints a word picture of the supernaturals, their "inner forms." Blessingway has precedence over all other chantways; its origin is placed just after Emergence from the underworld at the Emergence Place rim itself, before any chantway had been established. It occupies a central position in Navajo life, since it is concerned with the setting up of the Navajo world. For an excellent discussion of Blessingway and discussion of Navajo songs, see Gary Witherspoon, *Language and Art in the Navajo Universe*. Other helpful studies are Charlotte J. Frisbie, "Ritual Drama in the Navajo House Blessing Ceremony," in Frisbie, ed., *Southwestern Indian Ritual Drama*; Stephen C. Jett and Virginia E. Spencer, *Navajo Architecture* (University of Arizona Press, 1981); and Susan Kent, "Hogans, Sacred Circles, and Symbols: the Navajo Use of Space," in *Navajo Religion and Culture: Selected Views*, ed. David M. Brugge and Charlotte J. Frisbie (Museum of New Mexico Press, Santa Fe, 1982).

HASTEEN KLAH, *Navajo Creation Myth: The Story of Emergence*, recorded by Mary C. Wheelwright (Museum of Navajo Ceremonial Art, Santa Fe, 1942).

"Song of the Earth" is from *Hozhonji*, the Blessing Chant. The myth material is from the Creation Myth, or Story of the Emergence, of which there is more than one version. The great god Begochiddy, Fire God, Salt Woman, Coyote, First Man, and First Woman, prototypes of man, along with other creations, pass upward from the dark world to the Second or Blue World. They pass up to the Third or Yellow World, and then to this world, the Fourth or White. The path upward is shown in sandpaintings with the colors of the four worlds along the path. *Hozhonji* concerns "the blessing of the path of man, or of life itself," notes Wheelwright, "and all who are present at the final ceremony, whether initiate or not, are expected to walk along the path on the sandpainting." The ceremony used to be four days long, but now, according to Wheelwright, it is one day and one night.

Sahanahray and Bekayhozhon are the Holy Spirits of the Earth and Sky. They are connected with corn pollen and are shown with hands and feet clamped together, mouths too. This song, and all others in the volume, were sung by Hasteen Klah and recorded and transcribed by Harry Hoijer. For more on the singer, see Franc Johnson Newcomb, *Hasteen Klah: Navajo Medicine Man and Sand Painter* (University of Oklahoma Press, 1964). Also of interest is Paul Zolbrod, *Diné bahane: The Navajo Creation Story* (University of New Mexico Press, 1984), and Sheila Moon, *A Magic Dwells: A Poetic and Psychological Interpretation of the Navajo Emergence Myth* (Wesleyan University Press, 1970).

FATHER BERARD HAILE, *Prayer Stick Cutting in a Five-Night Navajo Ceremonial of the Male Branch of Shootingway* (University of Chicago Press, 1947).

The songs were dictated by White Singer of Chinle, Arizona, in 1929–30. The ceremony is exorcistic and purificatory, a "sanctification" process to render the patient "holy" or "immune to further attack from the supernatural who had previously interfered with his health." The ceremony is held in a hogan, and sandpaintings are used.

These songs are from the fourth and last day, when the patient is ritually bathed. Details of the songs become clear when thunder sandpaintings are consulted. Thus, in **"Bathing Song,"** "dark" refers to the east figure, while in each of the following three stanzas (not given here) "dark thunder" is replaced by "blue thunder" of the west, "yellow thunder" of the south, and "pink thunder" of the north. Sun bars always decorate the legs, trunk, and upper half of the wings of each creature, and other items are descriptions of the sandpainting. Father Haile notes that "song and painting delight in playing upon thunder's penchant for, and association with, clouds, sun bars, rainbows, rain sprays, and water. The song points out that through the bath thunder restores the patient from foot to head."

"Dawn Song" (in my version a running together of two related songs) is from a sequence nearer the end of the ceremony. It comes after a song about animals and birds, a kind of evocation. Coyote in legend is often connected with dawn and other phenomena of the cardinal points. The song draws on the story, widespread across America, of the eye juggler, in which Coyote tries to imitate Chickadee, who has the power to throw his eyes up into a tree and have them drop back into their sockets. When Coyote tries this, he fails and has his sockets filled with pine pitch.

David McAllester, in "Coyote's Song" (*Parabola* 4 [1980], 28–35), points out that while Coyote is "a maverick deity" among the Navajo, a "divine malcontent . . . misfit and demiurge," he is also "a little fearsome since he is also an embodiment of disorder and witchcraft." He has gifted the Navajo a legacy of songs, one of which, recorded in 1957, McAllester quotes and discusses. It is very similar to this song collected by Haile and is also from the Shootingway ceremonial. In McAllester's song, Coyote translates his ears into sacred feathers and names them as his power, which indeed they are. Coyote hears more than he sees since he's lost his eyes and had to replace them with yellow pebbles stuck in place with pine pitch, the result of coveting another's skill, or nature, and of his constant miscalculation.

KARL W. LUCKERT, *Navajo Mountain and Rainbow Bridge Religion*, vol. 1 of American Tribal Religions Series (Museum of Northern Arizona, Flagstaff, 1977).

Rainbow Bridge is a sandstone arch in southern Utah which was threatened by the waters of Lake Powell in 1971. Luckert was asked to document the significance of Rainbow Bridge in order to protect the sacred place.

"The Prayer of Slim Woman" of Kayenta was recorded by Hoffman Birney in 1927. It shows the Rainbow Bridge and Navajo Mountain religious complex was present in the 1920s.

At the end of the prayer I have tried to cover some of the semantic meanings of *honzo* (or *Hózhǫ́*) with "harmony," "happiness," "beauty."

CHARLOTTE J. FRISBIE, *Kinaaldá: A Study of the Navajo Girls' Puberty Ceremony* (Wesleyan University Press, 1967).

The ceremony was recorded on the Navajo Reservation of Chinle and Lukachukai, Arizona, 1963–64. The entire last night (and in some cases part of the first day) of the four-day and -night ceremony is spent in song. "Kinaaldá" varies in translation. Father Haile has it as "house, to sit," which relates to the segregation formerly used in menstruation. Changing Woman is the chief deity associated with the ceremony, which is part of the Blessingway ceremonial; "it ushers the girl into society," writes Frisbie, "invokes positive blessings on her, insures her health, prosperity, and well-being, and protects her from potential misfortune."

The Racing Songs follow the Dawn Songs, timed to coincide with the actual dawn. All Dawn Songs have four verses and all focus on one set of ideas, the appearance of the four deities: Dawn Boy in the East, Sunbeam Girl in the South, Evening Twilight Boy in the West, and Dipper Girl in the North. When the Dawn Songs are completed, the girl makes her final run and songs are sung (no set number, but between one and six). The menstruating girl might run up to three times, at dawn. She will run to the East, to and from the hogan, as fast as she can, from about two hundred yards to a quarter of a mile, before turning back in a sunwise, or clockwise, direction. Each run should be longer than the last, for long life, health, and happiness. Those of the girl's friends who want to run with her do so. Everyone is supposed to give the Kinaaldá shout to attract the attention of Changing Woman. The famous singer Frank Mitchell said the Racing Songs were first sung by Talking God for Changing Woman as she ran her daily morning races while she was growing up. It was Changing Woman who instructed the people to incorporate the songs into Kinaaldá, and the myth behind the ceremony is Changing Woman's Puberty Ceremony, the very first Kinaaldá (the girl is sometimes called "child of Changing Woman"). Changing Woman, who has many names, including White Shell Woman and Turquoise Woman, is the Earth. Black Jewel Girl is one of the initiate's titles, along with Turquoise Girl, White Shell Girl, and Abalone Girl.

From the many **Kinaaldá Racing Songs** I have selected two. Song I was sung on the final morning and Song II was sung on the first day, both by Blue Mule.

For a Navajo perspective on the ceremony, Shirley M. Begay's *Kinaaldá: A Navajo Puberty Ceremony* (Navajo Curriculum Center, Rough Rock Demonstration School, Arizona, 1983) is enlightening. It is unique in that it is the first account by a Navajo woman who has participated in the ceremony as an initiate. The book was written by a secondary school teacher primarily for Navajo students at secondary and junior college levels.

FATHER BERARD HAILE, *Love Magic and Butterfly People: The Slim Curly Version of the Ajiłee and Mothway Myths*, ed. Karl Luckert (Museum of Northern Arizona, Flagstaff, 1978).

The material in Haile's volume was recorded from 1930 to 1931. In Navajo legend, Pueblo virgins were highly prized and kept hidden in specially built houses with underground passages to water holes that sunlight could not penetrate. They were therefore called "non-sunlight-struck-ones."

The hero had been made fun of by the Hopis; "scrap picker" they'd called him when he was young. So this is a rags-to-riches story, as well as a story of revenge via sexual conquest—the hero seduces, marries, abandons, even causes the girls' deaths on his way to apotheosis as a fully sanctified shaman.

The solar hero is empowered by his Sun father and sets out to play his proper role as potent male: "to radiate sunlight," as Luckert phrases it, "into female existence." He continues: "The man gave new life in the form of solar light from Father Sky; the woman gave new life in the form of bodies from Mother Earth." He points out that the ecstatic experience of male shamans is made intelligible in the hunter with the metaphor of traveling on rainbow or sunbeam—in the line "at her ankle a rainbow will appear," "rainbow" could also be "sunbeam" or "sunray." The hero's identification with hallucinogenic or aphrodisiac plants remains a major theme in *ajiłee* songs (after this song there are others where the hero changes into a number of these plants, including "Jimsonweed Young Man"). The hero of the *ajiłee* myth was conceived by one of the flowering hallucinogenic Plant Girls.

Berard refers to *ajiłee* as "Prostitution Way." This term should be read in a broad "cosmic" sense: "It refers to the passionate reproductive behavior among all sexual beings," Luckert notes, "all possibilities and excesses."

HARRY HOIJER, *Chiricahua and Mescalero Apache Texts* (University of Chicago Press, 1938).

The closely related Chiricahua and Mescalero Apaches formerly lived in adjacent areas in Arizona and New Mexico. The Mescalero now live on the Mescalero Reservation in southern New Mexico, and the Chiricahua, after the surrender of Geronimo, shifted about until they settled on the Mescalero Reservation. Some were given land allotments near Apache, Oklahoma. **Songs of the Mountain Spirit**

Ceremony were collected in the summers of 1930 and 1931 and the spring of 1934. The texts were originally collected by Jules Henry from David Fatty, an old Chiricahua shaman.

I have only used two of the seventeen songs from this ceremony— enough, I hope, for the reader to get a sense of their intense hypnotic effect.

Most Chiricahua ceremonies are curative, performed by shamans who have obtained power from many sources, one of the most potent of which is the Mountain Spirits. These men dance to drive off the disease, and the shaman sings while they dance. The songs function as a message to the Mountain Spirits, a call to remind them to aid him since the Mountain Spirits themselves taught the shaman the songs. (The Mountain Spirits are associated with colors and directions, though the colors and directions vary.)

In Song VI, "he sings into my mouth" refers to the idea that when a person learns ceremonial songs from another, the teacher is said to "sing them into the mouth" of the pupil. This probably derives, Hoijer notes, from the practice of putting pollen into the mouth of the pupil four times at the end of apprenticeship. "Horns" in Song VII refers to the uprights on the masks worn by the masked dancers. They are here associated with yellow dust or pollen. "One can see in all directions" refers to the dancers who, because of the songs, are suffused with the abilities of the Mountain Spirits and can see evil and sickness and so drive them away.

GRENVILLE GOODWIN, *The Social Organization of the Western Apache* (University of Arizona Press, 1969; originally published in 1942).

"Song for a Baby Carrier," recorded by John Rope, is part of the traditional rite for making a carrier. It was used for a mother who had lost a baby or had a baby that was sickly in its regular cradle. Line 2 alludes to the frame, line 3 to the placing of the slats, and line 4 to the hood and the baby's head within. Line 5 refers to the loops alongside the frame for lacing the baby in, and line 6 refers to the lacing. Lines 8 and 9 are baby wrappings. "The whole," Goodwin notes, "is supposed to describe the making of the first baby carrier ever constructed." The man performing the ceremony sings the songs, and the woman repeats the words in a speaking voice.

RUTH M. UNDERHILL, *Papago Indian Religion* (Columbia University Press, 1946).

The songs were collected on the Sells Reservation in Arizona from 1931 to 1935. There are many songs in this book, and in Underhill's earlier *Singing for Power: The Song Magic of the Papago Indians of Southern Arizona* (University of California Press, 1938). Other Pima and Papago songs can be found in Frank Russell's *The Pima Indians*, ed. Bernard L. Fontana (University of Arizona Press, 1975; the book was first published in 1908), and Donald Bahr et al., *The Short, Swift Time of Gods on Earth: The Hohokan Chronicles* (University of California Press, 1994).

The Rainmaking Ceremony was held in July, at the beginning of the rainy season. It included fermenting and drinking liquor made from the fruit of the giant cactus. The name of the ceremony, "Náwai't," is from *nawai*, liquor, and *ta*, a suffix meaning "to make." "The idea," writes Underhill, "is that the saturation of the body with liquor typifies and produces the saturation of the earth with rain." The liquor did not have a high alcohol content, so lots had to be drunk, producing much vomiting, "a thorough purging."

Sexual license was often a feature of the festival, and certain unmarried women wandered from feast to feast, living with different men. Underhill notes that "such behavior may have been an old institution" and may have brought a special blessing. Many songs celebrate these women, whom Underhill terms "light women." Sometimes in the literature they are called "prostitutes" or "whores." Donald Bahr, in "Pima Oriole Songs" (in Brian Swann, ed., *Coming to Light*), calls them "whore women" but in correspondence informs me that "the pejorative, mercenary connotations do not apply." I have chosen the title **"Song of the Easygoing Women."**

"Speech Before Butchering the Deer" was spoken by the ceremonial orator at the beginning of the hunting season. Songs were also sung to summon the deer, and Underhill gives three of these cycles. The preparation and cooking of the deer was the occasion for song, dance, and oration to sanctify the food in a general cleansing ceremony. The deer was laid with its head to the west and was turned four times. After the deer was butchered, its tail was cut off and passed over each man's body in blessing. It seems in the oration that a straw image of the deer is made, but Underhill doesn't discuss this. The cosmic references indicate the mythical creation of the "first deer."

Deer and other animals could send sickness and disease as punishment for cruelty in the hunt and disrespectful treatment of remains.

Quail, for instance, could cause sore eyes. But animals also favor people with songs given in dream to be used to evoke their goodwill. Songs such as "**Quail Song**" told of the animals' habits so people would understand them and not cause them annoyance. (For more on this, see Donald Bahr et al., *Piman Shamanism and Staying Sickness* [University of Arizona Press, 1974].)

LEANNE HINTON AND LUCILLE J. WATAHOMIGIE, eds., *Spirit Mountain*: *An Anthology of Yuman Story and Song* (Sun Tracks/University of Arizona Press, 1984).

Medicine Songs are usually sung during curing sessions to the accompaniment of a rattle, but the "**Havasupai Medicine Song**" here was unaccompanied. This song, and others in the same section of the book, "can be thought of as partially improvised," notes Leanne Hinton. Dan Hanna was the singer, and he learned the song from Mark Hanna, a shaman. It can be sung by someone who is sick and wants to cure himself. A medicine song is received in a dream from a spirit; usually only professional shamans receive and sing curing songs, but this one is a *personal* curing song that can be sung by laymen to cure themselves. The song describes Havasupai Canyon (the Havasupais live in the Grand Canyon, in Arizona). At the end, the song refers to some boulders. When one lies down at this location they absorb sickness. The word translated "illness" is really, says Hinton, "a straying from the rightful road, the development of a disharmony with nature—which is what illness is defined to be." (Thanks to Leanne Hinton for permission to use her translation and for helping me with this version.)

CARLETON S. WILDER, *The Yaqui Deer Dance*: *A Study in Cultural Change*, Anthropological Papers no. 66, Smithsonian Institution, Bulletin no. 186 (Washington, D.C., 1963).

These songs were collected in 1939–40 in Pascua, Arizona, a village founded near Tucson by refugee and immigrant Yaquis from their Sonora homeland. The Deer Dance is performed at Easter.

The songs, each of which is sung a number of times by the three singers, are highly conventional in structure and theme. They use balancing and opposing structural elements and thought constructions, and I have attempted to retain some of those qualities. (Indeed, it would be hard not to use the bipartite form to show that the action taking place in the world of "reality" is duplicated throughout in a "supernatural" world.)

The songs do not form a strict sequence, and the number varies. They are, says Wilder, "songs to which the maso [deer dancer] dances." According to Larry Evers and Felipe S. Molina (*Yaqui Deer Songs/Maso Bwikam: A Native American Poetry* [University of Arizona Press, 1987]) they are the voice of *saila maso*, Little Brother Deer, who comes to dance for the Yaqui. The images of flowers predominate, and the references to clouds and water suggest an association of the deer with rain ceremony (one of the principal instruments to which the deer dancer dances is a water drum containing "flower water"). One can also surmise that the ceremony is for control over the deer.

In Song I, "where the sun rises" (along with, in later songs, "surrounded by flowers," "below the dawn," "home of the deer," "home of all animals") is used to translate *séye wáilo*, a mythical place. Song III presented difficulties to Wilder's informants, though it seems to be the singers calling the deer. This song is sung as the deer dancer comes out of the house directly into the ramada. The "flower water" refers to the mythological spring around which the deer dances and to the water in the water drum. There is no explanation of the bird's action in Song IV. The sound coming from the stick in Song V is the noise made by insects inside the wood. It is a signal for the people to gather together. The *maso* dances to the noise of sticks rasping together. Wilder notes of Song VI that "the entire translation of this section must be considered tentative." In Song VII, "flower stick" is not identified, and Wilder notes that he couldn't make a satisfactory transcription of Song VIII from the recording, "nor was it possible to get a satisfactory translation from my informants." In Song IX, "hoof belt" is a belt of deer-hoof rattles worn by the deer dancer, who also wears "cocoon anklets," cocoons filled with gravel and strung together on rawhide. In Song XII, the "cholla" is a kind of cactus. The final song, XIII, is sung about dawn, when the water used in the water drum is thrown up "to make rain," while another drummer beats his drum, imitating thunder. Other songs of the Deer Dance can be found in Muriel Thayer Painter, *With Good Heart: Yaqui Beliefs and Ceremonies in Pascua Village* (University of Arizona Press, 1986).

//

Grateful acknowledgment is made to the following for permission
to reprint previously published material:

CANADIAN MUSEUM OF CIVILIZATION: "Caribou Medicine Songs" from Diamond
Jenness, *The Sekani Indians of British Columbia*, Bulletin No. 84, Anthropologi-
cal Series No. 20, National Museum of Canada, Ottawa, 1937; "Siutinuaq's
Song," "Luke Uqualla's Song," "Arnaluaq's Song," "Qayutinuaq's Song,"
"Quuksun's Song," "Iqquqaqtuk's Song" from Beverly Cavanagh, *Music of the
Netsilik Eskimos: A Study in Stability and Change*, National Museum of Man
Mercury Series, Canadian Ethnology Service Paper No. 82, volume 2, Ottawa,
1982; Songs from Eskimo Point, No. 10, No. 16, from Ramon Pelinksi, Luke
Suluk, Lucy Amarook, *Inuit Songs from Eskimo Point*. National Museum of
Man Mercury Series, Canadian Ethnology Service, Paper No. 6, 1979; "Inupiat
Dance Songs I–III" from Thomas F. Johnson, *Eskimo Music by Region: A
Comparative Circumpolar Study*. National Museum of Man Mercury Series,
Canadian Ethnology Service, Paper No. 32, 1976; "Teasing Songs I, II" from
Maija M. Lutz, *Musical Traditions of the Labrador Coast Inuit*. National
Museum of Man Mercury Series, Paper No. 79, 1982; "Caribou Hunting Song,"
"Trapping Song," "Song for the Muskrat" from Richard J. Preston, *Cree Narra-
tive: Expressing the Personal Meaning of Events*, National Museum of Man
Mercury Series, Canadian Ethnology Service, Paper No. 30, Ottawa, 1975.
Reprinted by permission of Canadian Museum of Civilization.

COLUMBIA UNIVERSITY PRESS: "Hopi Butterfly Dance Song" from *Hopi Journal* by
A. M. Stephen. Copyright © 1936 by Columbia University Press. Reprinted
with permission of the publisher.

PETER GARCIA AND LINDA J. GOODMAN: "Prelude Dance," "Slow Standing Dance,"
"Fast Kneeling Dance," from "The Form and Function of the Basket Dance
of San Juan Pueblo" by Linda J. Goodman. Reprinted by permission.

MUSEUM OF NEW MEXICO: "San Juan Harvest Dance" and "One-Eyed Ford" from
Music and Dance of the Tewa Pueblos by Gertrude P. Kurath and Antonio
Garcia, Museum of New Mexico Research Records, no. 8, 1970. Reprinted by
permission.

MUSEUM OF NORTHERN ARIZONA: "The Prayer of Slim Woman" from *Navajo Mountain and Rainbow Bridge Religion* by Karl Luckert, vol. 1, American Tribal
Religions Series, 1977. "Hopi Virgins Seduced" from *Love Magic and Butterfly
People: The Slim Curly Version of the Ajilee and Mothway Myths* by Karl Luckert,
general editor, vol. 2, American Tribal Religions, 1978. Reprinted by permission
of the Museum of Northern Arizona, Flagstaff.

MUSICAL QUARTERLY AND OXFORD UNIVERSITY PRESS: "Iroquois Trotting Dance
Song" from *Antiphonal Songs of the Eastern Woodland Indians* by Gertrude P.
Kurath. Reprinted by permission of *Musical Quarterly* and Oxford University
Press.

SMITHSONIAN INSTITUTION PRESS: Excerpt from *Pawnee Music* by Frances Densmore,
Bulletin 93, 1929, Bureau of American Ethnology; excerpt from *Zuñi Ritual
Poetry* by Ruth L. Bunzel, Fourth Annual Report of the Bureau of American
Ethnology, 1929–30, 1932; excerpt from *Northern Ute Music* by Frances Dens-
more, Bulletin 75, 1922, Bureau of American Ethnology; excerpt from *The
Swimmer Manuscript: Cherokee Sacred Formulas and Medicinal Prescriptions* by
James Mooney, revised, completed and edited by Frans M. Olbrechts, Smithson-
ian Institution, Bureau of American Ethnology, Bulletin 99, 1932; excerpt from
The Yaqui Deer Dance: A Study in Cultural Change by Carleton S. Wilder.
Anthropological Papers No. 66, Bureau of American Ethnology, Bulletin 186,
1963. Reprinted by permission of Smithsonian Institution Press.

Other titles by Brian Swann available from the University
of Nebraska Press

Algonquian Spirit
Contemporary Translations of the Algonquian Literatures of North America

Voices from Four Directions
Contemporary Translations of the Native Literatures of North America

I Tell You Now
Autobiographical Essays by Native American Writers
with Arnold Krupat